PERIL
and
PROMISE

An Inquiry into Freedom of the Press

GERALD W. JOHNSON

GREENWOOD PRESS, PUBLISHERS
WESTPORT, CONNECTICUT

Library of Congress Cataloging in Publication Data

Johnson, Gerald White, 1890-
    Peril and promise; an inquiry into freedom of
the press.

    Reprint of the 1st ed. published by Harper &
Row, New York.
    1. Journalism--United States. 2. Liberty of
the press. I. Title.
[PN4867.J6 1974]   323.44'5   73-14034
ISBN 0-8371-7143-1

Originally published in 1958 by Harper & Brothers, New York

Reprinted with the permission of Harper & Row, Publishers, Inc.

Reprinted in 1973 by Greenwood Press,
a division of Williamhouse-Regency Inc.

Library of Congress Catalogue Card Number 73-14034

ISBN 0-8371-7143-1

Printed in the United States of America

CONTENTS

Acknowledgments

The substratum rather than the substance of this book is a series of lectures delivered by the writer as Walker-Ames Visiting Professor at the University of Washington in 1956; but the material has been revised and expanded to such an extent that to saddle responsibility for a single line on the University would be absurd. In any case, a Visiting Professor speaks to, but never for, the institution that is his host. Nevertheless, to this engagement, I owe the opportunity to undertake the work; so my thanks are due and heartily rendered to the University, to its School of Communications, and especially to the Director of the School, Henry Ladd Smith, Ph.D., and his staff, whose skill and courtesy not only lightened the guest's labor but made his stay in Seattle a delight at the time and a radiant memory since.

GERALD W. JOHNSON

Baltimore
February, 1957

vii

PERIL and PROMISE

FOREWORD

The modern world is sick. On that proposition philosophers of all shades of opinion, from Bertrand Lord Russell to Pogo the Possum, inclusive, are agreed although there is no unanimity on the diagnosis of the ailment. Communism, Capitalism, Fascism, Socialism, Republicanism, Democracy and democracy are all accused by one or another of the political quacks that infest the premises, and each can argue *post hoc ergo propter hoc* in eloquent defense of his thesis. Probably all are right. Each of these things may be to some extent a malaise contributing to the discomfort of the modern generation. But probably all are wrong in that none touches the underlying dystrophy that renders us vulnerable to every infection that floats upon the tainted wind.

Probably all are wrong in another respect. It is not certain that *all* the modern world is sick. To narrow the thing down to more nearly manageable proportions, it is not certain that the whole American population is sick. It is not necessary that everyone should be ill to give an impression of an all-pervasive morbidity; twenty per cent will suffice, provided the fifth includes all the loud-mouthed. When the articulate are sick their regurgitations are noisy enough to obliterate any small sounds indicative of health among four-fifths of the population, so betraying the observer into the belief that he contemplates a dying nation.

The observations that follow, accordingly, should be read not as applying to every American citizen without exception, indeed not as applying, in the writer's opinion, to a majority, but only to those who are definitely, blatantly, unmistakably ailing. Unfortunately they include many millions, perhaps as many as forty out of the one hundred and sixty millions that comprise the population. Obviously, this is a situation that is already serious and that may become desperate with great rapidity unless strong measures are taken, and promptly. Yet strong measures are folly unless they are preceded by an adequate and accurate diagnosis of the basic trouble.

The symptoms are familiar to the most superficial observer. They include disbelief in the foundations of the republic, a disbelief that may range in intensity all the way from a slight skepticism as to the practicality of the Bill of Rights, to black despair of the future of democracy. This expresses itself in a progressive hostility to new ideas and an increasing confidence in the efficacy of what the Chinese call "brain-washing" accompanied by an increasing determination that the intellectual laundry shall be manned exclusively by qualified and authorized personnel bonded for the faithful performance of duty.

FOREWORD

So we have a rash of test oaths of all kinds, of security programs, of un-American Activities committees, of McCarthys and Cohns and Schines, of book-burnings, of library purges, of censorships of bookstores and magazine racks, of raids upon the schools and colleges, and of a disposition to bracket scientists, especially physicists, slightly above pickpockets and slightly below fortunetellers on the scale of personal integrity. We do not suspect the learned doctors of a propensity to steal our purses. We suspect them of a propensity to steal our brains, or, worse, of introducing into our brains effervescent ideas that will cause them to swell up and burst. In brief, we are hagridden by a hideous fear that the average American will somehow hear what is not good for him to hear, with disastrous results.

How the ailing American has managed to get into this fix is the subject of endless debate among the pundits who have, as before stated, advanced every kind of explanation from Communism to Calvinism, but have agreed on none. Yet there is a perfectly obvious one that nobody has advanced, perhaps because it is as unpopular as it is obvious.

This explanation is that the average American is convinced, in his heart of hearts, that he is getting away with murder. We live too well, considering the state of the rest of the world, and we are haunted by dread that at any day the rest of the world may realize it and expose us. Doubtless it is, for the most part, a subconscious fear. Under questioning it is likely that most of us would deny it, quite sincerely. I may

3

be unconquerably persuaded that my particular virtues and talents are rewarded with shameful scantiness, but how about Joe Doakes, who lives down the block? In all candor, isn't the fellow living in a better house, and wearing better clothes, and eating better food than his energies and abilities would entitle him to under any well-regulated scheme of things?

In the urban population there is certainly a widespread opinion that the farmers are getting a great deal more than their due, and rural dwellers are no less firmly convinced that city men are living a far softer life than they deserve. Office workers and executives, when they are frank, complain that organized labor is scandalously overpaid. All of us know that the American population, as a whole, enjoys a standard of living far higher than that of the most favored nations in other parts of the world.

We are aware, too, that we didn't do it. We are indeed applying energy and skill to the available materials, but the enormous accumulation of capital that renders our labor profitable beyond all precedent was the work of grandfather, and he's dead. More than that, the original American had an untouched continent to exploit, and we have not. So how long we can keep it up is a question that is nagging at all our minds. We hope that the pace can be maintained indefinitely, but we fear that at any moment something—nobody knows exactly what, so it may be anything—will happen to upset the apple cart and reduce us to the economic level of people who are less fortunate but, we know in our hearts, quite as deserving as we are.

This would account for the frenetic opposition to any further exploration of the ideas underlying our system of government. It would account for the equation of criticism with treason. It would account for the current disposition to regard research as attainted of moral turpitude and therefore to be held within the narrowest possible limits. It would account for the propensity to resent a lifted eyebrow with a violence once reserved for a slap in the face. And, of course, it would account for the dismal pessimism of the nobility and gentry.

Naturally, such a state of mind affords an ideal field of operations for frauds and charlatans of every conceivable variety. A man with a low opinion of himself is unlikely to have an exalted opinion of his neighbors; and if his self-dissatisfaction is no superficiality, but is so deeply buried as hardly to rise into his conscious mind at all he is certain to take a pessimistic view of the character and capabilities of the generality of mankind.

With such conditioning he becomes the natural prey of smooth operators with a genius for ferreting out and playing upon suspicion, distrust and anxiety. Gentry who are skilled at taking our minor virtues and converting them into gyves for our wrists foment ordinary prudence into paralyzing terror, healthy skepticism into poisonous cynicism, an inclination to make haste slowly into stolid inertia, firmness into stubbornness. Uncertain of our own direction we become, in Reisman's term, "other-directed," pawns, not to say chattels of outsiders.

There is no idiocy so fantastic that it cannot be imposed upon men in this state. To persuade them that the moon is made of green cheese is nothing; they can even be persuaded that Communism is a conspiracy, despite the obvious fact that if Communism is a conspiracy a steam calliope is the whisper of a zephyr and a four-alarm fire is a candle in the window. Communism is a fighting faith—a form of devil worship, if you please, but no more a conspiracy than Islam was a conspiracy when Amru was sweeping from the Nile to the Atlantic, or than Protestantism was when Gustavus Adolphus was wrecking Wallenstein at Lützen.

Men in this state can be led not merely into idiocy, but even into flat heresy. They can be persuaded that the greasiest politician who can bribe, steal, or swindle his way into a seat in Congress becomes, by the success of his criminal conduct, endowed with the authority of the Searcher of Hearts to examine the consciences of free men. It is forbidden to render unto Caesar the things that are God's; how much more stern must be the prohibition against rendering them, not to a formidable emperor, but to any person who gets elected to Congress, no matter whether he be a statesman, or some verminous ward heeler with the manners of an orangutan and the intelligence of a cockroach!

To put it in a nutshell, men in this state have gone far

toward losing the capacity for self-government. They may not—indeed, they never do—realize it, but their political activities are no longer the result of their own choice, they are the response of puppets to strings pulled by astute manipulators.

These are sick men, beyond peradventure, but to assume that they can be restored to health by protecting them from infection is to assume that the world can be made aseptic, which is more irrational than the wildest phantasm conjured up by political delirium. The moral and spiritual anemia that laid them open to infection, that is, the collapse of the inner defenses, is the basis of the trouble, and the treatment entails a long regimen, not any quick surgery or miracle drugs.

The ultimate aim must be to convince the ailing American that he is, potentially at least, considerably more decent than his subconscious suggests. He is not really a dog, he is the highest of the primates, endowed with capacities not demonstrably shared by the brute creation. Among these is the ability to maintain as dirty a mind as his sinful propensities make it, for his brain cannot be washed without his consent. Granted that if he were delivered to Chinese torturers they could by a combination of starvation and their diabolic arts reduce him physically to a level at which he would consent to anything; yet a brain tumor or certain kinds of skull fracture may do the same thing, that is, destroy the personality without killing the body. This, however, is irrelevant as long as we are not in the hands of Chinese torturers.

The characteristic of the sort of person called, if you follow Riesman, "inner-directed," or, if you follow the older nomenclature, "a freeman," is that in deciding upon a course of action he chooses between alternatives without reference to any exterior pressure. Perhaps this apparent freedom is illusory. Perhaps the behaviorists are right, and all our choices are determined by inner pressures of which we are only dimly aware or completely oblivious. Let the psychologists of the different schools fight that out among themselves, for the answer whatever it be is of no value to the man faced with a concrete, immediate problem. Justifiably or not, he *thinks* he is free to vote either Democratic or Republican, to support Eisenhower's foreign policy or oppose it, to denounce the Bricker Amendment or approve it; and as long as he thinks he is free the process of making a decision is as laborious as if he were free.

That labor is made more complicated and more onerous if to its intrinsic difficulty is added a nagging suspicion of his own competence to judge fairly when all the facts are laid before him and the arguments of all sides are heard with equal attention. The superstitious reverence that Americans attach to an ill-defined influence commonly termed "propaganda" adds to their burden when choices must be made, for this delusion of the omnipotence of propaganda flatly contradicts the most cheerful of the maxims upon which the American system is based—Jefferson's dictum that "error of opinion may be tolerated where reason is left free to combat it."

FOREWORD

It is almost unheard-of for a modern American to reject the dictum in principle, but in practice he is ridden by an inextinguishable doubt that reason is often, if ever, left free to combat error. Reason, he feels, is commonly overwhelmed, smothered and rendered impotent by the volume and devilish cleverness of propaganda, so the observation of Jefferson, however true, is actually irrelevant to the existing situation.

This applies with especial force to the intellectuals, no doubt because their wider reading gives them greater familiarity with the diversity of contending opinions. The squarehead, laying the flattering unction to his soul that he has only one, or at most two or three liars to watch and avoid, may live more or less at ease in Zion; but the egghead, aware that liars, like sorrows, "come not single spies but in battalions," lives in the wretched expectation of being overwhelmed by numbers. Certain it is that the incessant threnodies for the American mind, debauched by propaganda and especially by the open and aboveboard propaganda represented in paid advertising, are fabricated almost exclusively by intellectuals, seldom by squares. Phi Beta Kappa, not Rotary, is their fount.

It is true that one very eminent egghead, Woodrow Wilson, discovered and explained the automatic check that propaganda imposes upon its own career. While the problem of our southern neighbor was still his chief worry as President, he said that he arrived at the truth about Mexican affairs "by balancing lies." The squarehead undoubtedly employs the same method to arrive at an approximation of the truth about cigarettes, automobiles and electric refrigerators, which explains why the American people, enduring the most terrific barrage of propaganda-as-advertising to which any nation was ever subjected, are not gulled to a conspicuous extent as regards the quality of the goods they purchase. Swindled they may be, and in a very large way at that, but the method employed is that of persuading them that they desire things they really do not want, not that of trapping them into buying shoddy goods.

It would seem, therefore, that the incessant and poignant sounds of woe being emitted by the intellectual lamenting the debauchery of the American mind by the irresistible force of advertising are somewhat overdone. This is almost, if not quite, the only field in which the battle of ideas rages without let or hindrance. True, government interposes to forbid two of the three categories of mendacity and looks with a fishy eye on the third. An advertiser risks the pains and penalties of the law if he tells lies, or damned lies, and has to be a bit wary about how he handles statistics. But short of demonstrable prevarication, the field is open and the American public is attacked with every resource that the wizards of propaganda can think up. Far from being distrustful of novelty, advertising holds it to be the pearl beyond price, and the genius whose thinking ranges furthest and fastest is chiefest of all.

Yet it is precisely in this field that the success of the American system of conducting affairs is least open to doubt.

FOREWORD

The general level of quality of the goods on the shelves of American retail stores is higher than that in any other nation; there is not even a question except as to certain lines of luxury goods and some specialties whose excellence is attributable either to jealously guarded trade secrets, or to geographic and climatic advantages possessed by the producing countries. Doubtless the wines of France, the gems of Amsterdam, the carpets of Shiraz are supreme; but what the typical American housewife takes home in her shopping bag is generally agreed to be better than what a housewife on the corresponding economic level takes home in any other country.

If the supposed omnipotence of propaganda were a fact this would not be the case. American goods would be the shoddiest in the world if the power of publicity were able to deceive the average man and keep him deceived; but the historical fact is that the psychological pressure exerted by the maker of one automobile has been counteracted and neutralized by the psychological pressure exerted by his rivals so that the resultant of the forces is so near immobility that the individual preferences of the customer are commonly decisive.

In 1787 James Madison expressed the opinion that an analogous play of forces in the political realm could be relied on to maintain the stability of the republic. Faction, said Madison, is an inevitable development in a democracy, as certainly as special interests are in an economy, but when the democracy is numerically and geographically very large, factions will arise in great numbers and none is likely to obtain dominance over the whole country.

The influence of factious leaders may kindle a flame within their particular States, but will be unable to spread a general conflagration through the other States. . . . A rage for . . . any improper or wicked project will be less apt to pervade the whole body of the Union than a particular member of it; in the same proportion as such a malady is more likely to taint a particular county or district, than an entire State.*

Even if one such faction should succeed in capturing the central government for the moment it cannot retain dominance long, for the others will combine to pull it down. A plurality of opposing forces, operating simultaneously, results in equilibrium.

The history of the republic to date has sustained Madison's logic. It is fatuous to assume that the reason we have never produced a Hitler or a Stalin is that the very air that Americans breathe is fatal to tyrants; what is fatal to tyrants is, and has always been, here as elsewhere, a well-aimed brick flung by the hand of some rival aspirant to tyranny. Even as in a welter of advertising whose fraudulence is often of a very high proof we have established a market whose general level of excellence is unsurpassed, so in a welter of political contention assaying at least nineteen hundredweight to the ton pure buncombe, we have established a political system that has now outlasted all others that existed in 1789—for

* *The Federalist*, Number 10 (Madison).

FOREWORD

Great Britain did not emerge into its democratic phase until after the Reform Bill of 1832.

The plain inference is that in economics and politics, both systems of thought expressed in action, true stability is not that of a monolith, but that of a gyroscope, which can be tilted, but inexorably returns to its original plane. Or, to vary the metaphor, the peace that endures longest is to be sought precisely at the point where the battle of ideas rages with the most unrestrained fury. This is a concept that challenges all orthodoxies, religious, political, economic, social; it is therefore intolerable to some minds and can be assimilated by many others only with great difficulty. It is palatable, in fact, only to the temperament that for the lack of a more exact term we call optimistic, that is to say, the type of mind whose bent is to see in prospective action its promise of gain, rather than its threat of loss. Both are present, as a rule, in any proposed action, so it is idle to contend that one view is more realistic than the other; and the disposition of a specific individual to incline to one rather than the other seems to be determined as much by his biological inheritance as by his experience and environment.

But, so the astrologers assure us, "the stars incline, they do not compel." Assuming that each is a rational man, an innate conservative may be driven by the facts of life to take, on occasion, a liberal attitude; and, by the same forces, your born liberal may at times be impelled into the conservative camp. It is probable that, like the Ethiopian of

Scripture, neither can change his basic coloration, but this does not mean that men are irretrievably committed to a specific point of view under all circumstances and on all occasions. Which is to say, the basic policy of the American republic is still debatable.

Very superficial study of our political history is enough to suggest—it is a temptation to say flatly, "to establish" that concentration upon the promise, rather than upon the threat implied in future action has been the correct course for this nation at most times. This has been inherent in the situation. The republic proclaimed in 1776 and permanently organized in 1789 was an experiment in the applied science of government. Democracy had been tried repeatedly, but never before in this particular form. The earlier experiments had not been encouraging; the percentage of failure, in point of fact, had been exactly one hundred. It was evident, therefore, that in America everything depended upon the form, and the form was without precedent.

The experimental method proceeds by first forming a hypothesis and then testing it by every means that ingenuity can suggest. It is of the essence of sound experimentation to omit no test that has never been tried, so the novelty of an idea is its strongest recommendation, assuming, of course, that it does not involve action that obviously would destroy the apparatus. The hypothesis, in the case of the American experiment, is stated in the Declaration of Independence as

the theory that governments are instituted among men to secure certain inalienable rights that the individual holds, not
by purchase, nor by conquest, nor by guile, but as an endow-
ment from the Creator. The apparatus by which the hypothesis was to be tested was set up in the Constitution of the
United States.

It follows that the dominant mood of the American people
as a political organization has been, and should have been,
the expectation of gain rather than the fear of loss. Starting
with nothing to lose, we could not take any other attitude.
By the same token, the utmost hospitality to ideas was the
only rational policy for us to adopt, since only through the
conception of new ideas could a new form of government have
any chance of success. But an idea that is not expounded might
as well never have been conceived, as far as government
is concerned, and the exposition of any really novel idea
must, in the beginning, bear all the stigmata of heresy; so
freedom of speech and of the press was necessary to successful
conduct of the experiment and any restriction upon either
was justifiable only to the extent that it was essential to
secure the safety of life and property.

The hypothetical entity currently termed "Americanism"
is neither life nor property and is entitled to no protection as
against freedom of speech and of the press. The suggestion
that it may take precedence was vigorously repudiated by
the third President. "If there be any among us who would
wish to dissolve this Union [Secessionists, for example] or to

15

change its republican form [Communists, Fascists, Royalists, White Supremacists] let them stand undisturbed," he said, "as monuments of the safety with which error of opinion may be tolerated where reason is left free to combat it." In short, un-American activities were to be scorned as idiotic, not punished as criminal.

Yet Jefferson was not by nature a man to suffer fools gladly. He advised that course because, and only because, he knew that every novel idea looks idiotic when it is first propounded. Its novelty assures that. Jefferson shared the knowledge that is soon gained by every scientific experimenter that ninety-nine out of every hundred new ideas are in fact idiotic, but must all be accepted for examination in order not to miss the hundredth idea that is sound and whose value more than compensates for the labor of examining and rejecting the ninety-nine.

Following the method of subjecting our new form of government to every imaginable criticism, the ninety-nine forms that were silly as well as the one that was wise, we have done very well, so far. Democracy, that total failure up to 1789, under its new form has been made to work for a hundred and sixty-eight years—not perfectly, of course, but well enough to transform a thin string of backwoods settlements along the Atlantic coast into the richest and most powerful nation in the world today. The material success of the United States is beyond debate; and some among us hold that it has not been a moral failure, even though its moral success has been by no means as dazzling. Justice and freedom do not prevail among us, but neither have they been totally extinguished; at least we continue to pay lip service to both and in limited measure to grant both to all classes of men.

Nevertheless, it is as true of nations as of men that "time and chance happeneth to them all." Systems have their day and become outmoded. It is logically conceivable that the time has come when the United States should view every proposed action with distrust, more impressed by the fear of loss than by the hope of gain.

Yet how is this to be determined except by maintaining the free play of ideas in order that the best may, as Justice Holmes put it, gain acceptance in the market place? If the backward look is best, so be it; but we cannot know it is best until we have become familiar with the forward look. It is possible that the experiment that has been in process for the better part of two hundred years is on the verge of conclusive success; but it is not yet demonstrated, and until the demonstration is beyond question the apparatus should not be dismantled. On the contrary, the closer we approach success, the more careful we should be to make sure that the apparatus is working as it was meant to work.

Furthermore, there is the disturbing possibility that the success of the American experiment, like the success of most scientific investigations, will only clear the way to a vaster experiment that will involve more time and more labor. The position of the American people today is in some respects as ambiguous as it was in 1789. We are—somewhat to our surprise and very much to our discomfort—in a position of leadership of the free nations, and there are many indications that we may be called on to guide, even though we may not conduct, a second experiment in the art of government, this one involving half the world.

Obviously, no such enterprise can be conducted successfully by a people whose thinking has become stereotyped and whose ideas are confined to copy-book maxims handed down from the past. On the contrary, as the dimensions of the task exceed those of our first endeavor, by so much the greater will be the strain on our ingenuity, resourcefulness and intellectual daring. If it took fast thinking and a great deal of it to bring self-government to its present level in the United States, we need not delude ourselves with the hope that to bring a free world to a comparable degree of stability will call for slower thinking and less of it.

The Constitution of the United States underwent its narrowest escape from destruction in 1861, but it has been gravely threatened in three other crises—in 1814, when New England threatened to secede, in 1833 when South Carolina tried Nullification, and in 1929 when the economic system collapsed. Each of these crises was precipitated, not by a foreign foe, but by the fact that in each instance an important segment of the American people had lost intellectual contact with the realities of the situation then existing. For one reason or another the free flow of ideas was blocked and, instead of by creative thinking, people were living, as Robert Louis Stevenson remarked, "mostly by catch-phrases."

If it is indeed the case, as it seems to be, that the task of leading the way toward a world governed by law rather than by military strength is devolving upon the American people, it is only too clear that now is the time when we can least afford to abandon the exploration of ideas. For if the clash of opinion was essential to the building of a great national state, it is not reasonable to suppose that it will play a less important part in the establishment of an orderly world. Most certainly the leader in that endeavor cannot afford to make any such assumption.

Creative thinking may be the product of individual genius, but there is no doubt whatever that it is stimulated by the clash of contending ideas. Genius cannot be produced on command, but talent which, within limits, can serve as a substitute for it, is, if not created, at least brought out and developed by the battle of ideas. It follows that the rapid circulation of ideas produces the most favorable situation for the appearance of either genius or talent.

In the United States the most important element in the circulatory system of ideas is the press. As regards rapidity of circulation, this statement may be confined to the periodical press, disregarding book publishing. It follows that the intellectual health of the nation depends upon the proper functioning of that element of the system.

The periodical press is the circulatory system of information, that is to say, news, as well; but as to that part of its function a glance at any issue of any first-class American newspaper will reassure most observers. There is no denying that some newspapers have "slanted," which is to say, distorted news, and some few have actually suppressed news; but the American press is, I believe, as free of both faults as the press of any other nation in the world, and in this respect is greatly superior to most. Certainly the volume of news presented to the American reader is unmatched anywhere else.

It is the free circulation of opinion concerning which some question arises. Many American journalists take the view that opinion is not news, unless it is the opinion of someone approaching in importance the President or a movie star. What seems to be heretical opinion is emphatically not news; it is propaganda, which is a sort of anti-news to be kept out of the paper at any cost. Sometimes this is true; but it is a dangerous attitude, not to the press alone, but also to our system of representative government, and the extent to which it pervades journalism is a legitimate subject of inquiry by laymen.

I THE PERIL

At the Columbia University Bicentennial celebration in 1955 an acute observer of modern trends, Adlai E. Stevenson, made a remark that attracted little attention at the time, but that becomes more sensational the more one meditates upon it. He said, "I wonder if today mass manipulation is not a greater danger than economic exploitation; if we are not in greater danger of becoming robots than slaves."

Logicians may protest that this is vain repetition, since a robot is a slave, but ordinary men whose minds are less precise have no difficulty in understanding what Mr. Stevenson meant. To their way of thinking, a robot is definitely more than a slave. A slave is a man in chains, whereas a robot is a creature without chains but with built-in slavery. A robot is, from the standpoint of the master, a vastly improved slave, seeing that he guards himself, thereby saving the master the expense of Simon Legree's pay.

A generation ago the typical American would have dismissed the suggestion that we may become robots as the product of a perfervid imagination comparable to Mary Shelley's

succeed. It accordingly encourages distrust of one's own reason; and a man distrustful of his own ability to recognize truth when it is presented to his eyes is necessarily distrustful of his own liberty to direct his acts in accordance with reason. To encourage this distrust is precisely the aim of the Communists, which means that the presumed defense against them is actually playing their game.

If manacles and fetters of actual, material steel were fastened upon us, we should be prisoners who might be driven to slave labor; but we should not yet be slaves. The Communists discovered that in the recent case of Hungary. For the man in chains there is always hope that a moment may come when the strength of the guards will ebb or their attention relax, which is the moment to burst the bonds. A nation enchained is not yet a nation reduced to the purposes of any form of despotism, Communism included; the only complete success of despotism comes when the conquered nation's will to be free is broken. Anything that tends to break the will to be free is of assistance to any form of despotism. Even fear of Communism so hysterical that it drives us to sacrifice essential liberty is of service to Communism because it breaches the one really stout defense against every form of tyranny.

But all this, be it noted, is in the realm of opinion. Factual information is the basis of opinion, but it is not the thing itself. There is much reason to believe that the American people, in the mass, are the best-informed people in the world, as far as factual knowledge goes; and if it were certain that their opinions are as sturdy as their information is comprehensive there would be no need for such alarm as is indicated by the existence of un-American Activities committees, and incessant investigations of movies, colleges, foundations and newspapers.

The existence of these things and their toleration if not active support by a large proportion, perhaps although not certainly a majority of the people, is conclusive evidence that a great many Americans are convinced that their neighbors are thinking foul thoughts; which implies, of course, that a great many Americans are thinking foul thoughts themselves. They are secretly renouncing liberty because, being unworthy of it themselves, they are certain that their neighbors are even less worthy. We are building up an inward tolerance of slavery that leads toward a preference for it; and if we reach that state we shall inevitably succumb to some form of despotism. We shall be fortunate if it proves to be no worse a form than Communism; it might be Ku Kluxism, the American version of Hitlerism.

It follows that a grave responsibility rests upon those Americans whose professional work touches in any way upon the formation or direction of public opinion. In the broadest sense, no doubt, this includes every American since there is no man or woman, barring hermits and the certified insane, who does not exert some influence in social intercourse; but in a narrower sense there are three groups whose energies are devoted in major part to that kind of work. Mr. Stevenson, as a lawyer and politician, represents one of the most important of these groups. The others are educators, including theologians to the extent that instruction in mundane affairs is one of their duties, and journalists, including in that group practitioners in all media of communication, and, if it be no sacrilege to include them among journalists, such philosophers as admit that social ecology is a component of ontology.

The jurisconsults, the divines and the learned doctors may answer for themselves; the concern of this book is with the journalists, and with the conditions making for and against the adequate discharge of their responsibility for the maintenance of a healthy public opinion in this country. In this field the press remains by long odds the most important force since it is the medium of record. Radio and television may exert a very powerful momentary influence; television, in particular, inasmuch as it brings to bear visual as well as verbal argument, may at the moment of impact be more powerful than the press. But when it comes to the studied decisions on which the more important public acts are based, the medium of record comes into its own. The words of radio and television are words in the air; but the printed word may be reread and examined to determine its exact meaning. So it is the basis of cool, unemotional and permanent decision.

The conditions under which the press, and especially the newspaper press works are, therefore, affected with a public interest in a high degree. Newspapers are the source of the great bulk of our information, not only as to what is being done in the world but also as to what is being thought in the world; and this is true regardless of status and occupation. The grease monkey in the filling station is no more dependent on the newspapers for his current information than is the savant in his book-lined study. The capacity of the press to provide that information unadulterated is accordingly a matter superseding any class or special interest, since a newspaper press hampered by either prohibitions or inhibitions is of small help in creating and maintaining the climate of opinion in which liberty can survive.

The dilemma of the plain citizen is that as the world is constituted he simply cannot do without journalism, politics, or religion.* All are loaded with dynamite, yet he must have them all; so his problem is not how to get rid of any, but how to make use of all three without being blown up, since it is by deft use of the three that the American enters the estate of a free man.

Few who have lived to the years of discretion will deny

---

* Before you have time to say it, let me confess that I know the literal truth of the assertion that

  We may live without poetry, music and art;
  We may live without conscience and live without heart;
  We may live without friends; we may live without books;
  But civilized man cannot live without cooks,

so the statement above is, if you insist, metaphysical; one may indeed survive without an idea in the world; but such a survivor does not rise to the level of a plain citizen; he is a non-voter.

that by the time a man's education has proceeded to the college level he knows that freedom is a relative term. All men are controlled; if not by a slave driver armed with a blacksnake whip, or with a knout, or with a Tommy gun, then by the invisible but none the less efficient slave drivers of his own beliefs, his passions and his prejudices. What we call the free man is only relatively free; he is merely one who has somehow retained the power to choose among compulsions and to submit to none but those of his own inner being; and he who is most completely free is one who chooses even among those inner drives, and bows only to such as seem most consistent with reality and reason.

It follows, therefore, that the highest attainable freedom is contingent upon the fullest and most accurate information since reality and reason hang upon information; so those agencies whose function is the dissemination of information are crucial. It is undeniable that the three lines of endeavor that I have mentioned do overlap to an important extent; but journalism alone is concerned almost equally with public affairs, spiritual affairs and educational, which is to say, cultural affairs. The journalist, in short, is a generalist as opposed to a specialist; which implies that he has wider opportunities, whether for good or for evil, than either the politician or the educator. The inescapable inference is that he will bear watching more than either of the others.

Yet in the same measure that it is socially dangerous his function is socially necessary. It is not that of a mere narrator.

THE PERIL

It is all very well to talk of strict objectivity in presentation of the news, but the idea that complete objectivity is attainable is sheer nonsense. The volume of news in the modern world is beyond the capacity of any newspaper, even the *New York Times*, to print, and if it were printed it would be far beyond the capacity of any human mind to absorb. The news is never complete, it is representative; and determination of what is fairly representative is not objective, it is highly subjective and cannot be anything else.

It is the fashion in the craft to deprecate what is called "personal journalism," by which we usually mean journalism with a personal bias frankly admitted. Strictly speaking, the expression "personal journalism" is a tautology, because if it is journalism at all it is bound to be personal. The choice of what to print and how to print it has to be made by some person and that person's character and intelligence will slant the news. The only periodical publication I have ever seen with no slant at all is the annual *Statistical Abstract of the United States* which prints every figure available; and that is not journalism.

This inescapable condition floors a strict logician. If all news is inevitably slanted, he says, then the cause is already lost and we are intellectual prisoners of the press. This would be true if man were strictly logical, but he isn't. The human mind is erratic. The little ball that spins on a roulette wheel is hardly less predictable, which is what makes life, not in Mr. Huxley's "brave new world," but in the cowardly old world, endurable and often charming.

The American mind is actually much tougher than many of us can believe. What makes us so sad about it all is usually a blind spot in our own eyes that prevents us from seeing the merit in a man or a proposition that appeals to the people. For any great popular success has always some merit of some kind, even when the omniscient press cannot see it.

In his autobiography former President Truman says that in 1948 he analyzed the thirty-six presidential elections held up to that time and discovered that a heavy majority of the press had supported the winner in exactly eighteen. This convinced him that press support is not decisive, which was all he needed to know in 1948, so he dropped it there.

But he might have drawn another inference. Most careful students of American political history are agreed that in the whole number of elections the popular choice has been the better choice more often than not.* My own opinion is that this was the case in at least twenty-five of the thirty-six elections that Truman studied. Remember, if you please, that the voter could not choose from the whole field; he was restricted to a very small group of formal candidates—eight in 1952, nine in 1956—and of these the practical choice usually lay between the candidates of the two major parties. The voters have simply had to make the best of it. In the second election of Grant, for instance, the people's choice seems to have been

* See, for example, *They Also Ran*, Irving Stone's entertaining study of losers.

a bad one; but the alternative was Horace Greeley, and although Grant was incompetent, Greeley would have been fabulously incompetent. So even a bad choice may be better than the alternative.

On the face of the figures then, the press, splitting its support evenly between winners and losers, cannot have been right more than half the time, whereas history has justified the choice of the people at least two-thirds of the time. In the case of presidential politics two things seem fairly clear: first, press support has not, as a rule, been decisive; and, second, press judgment has not, as a rule, been as good as popular judgment.

Historically, then, the manipulation of public opinion by journalism has not been, in presidential politics, either conspicuously wise or conspicuously successful. The two most startling failures among Presidents, Grant and Harding, both had massive press support. The most startlingly successful of all Presidents, James K. Polk, had almost none; indeed, the all but unanimous inquiry of the press after his nomination was, "Who is James K. Polk?" Today we can answer, "He is the only President who ever scored five hits out of five times up." His announced program was to acquire California, settle the Oregon dispute, lower the tariff, establish a sub-treasury, and retire at the end of his first term, and he did all five, a record that still stands.

So it may be said that American reaction to the dictates of journalism has been anything but submissive, which is ample reason for refusing to become hysterical over supposed danger to liberty in this direction. Yet there must be a first time for everything, and it is beyond dispute that in recent years the organization of journalism has undergone profound changes in the direction of centralization and perfection of control; and it is possible that these may improve its efficiency in converting Americans into robots.

The question, therefore, is not closed by the historical fact that the power of the press up to this time has been far from absolute. The probable effect of recent changes must be taken into account and these deserve consideration, both from the standpoint of the craftsman, in order that he may fully understand his trade, and also from that of the reader, in order that he may know how to resist undue pressures.

The most spectacular changes in journalism in the last generation have been caused by the immense technical advances in means of communication. For instance, radio has abolished the newspaper extra and altered the nature of the scoop. Every newspaper story dealing with current events is now more or less in the nature of a follow-up story, because the flash has already gone out over the radio. From the standpoint of the press this is an improvement, for breakneck speed inevitably multiplies inaccuracies.

It has also eliminated the factor of luck from the scoop. It still exists, but today it is either the result of a favor, such as an exclusive interview, or of long and laborious investigation. This ignores those instances in which it is the result of villainy, such as a breach of confidence or a theft of documents. That isn't journalism, that is crime, and we are here considering a lawful occupation.

A digression may be permitted here for the benefit of a hypothetical non-professional reader who does not understand why many newspapermen regard the exclusive interview granted by a public official as being, if not quite a crime, yet the next thing to it. First, the exclusive interview is a favor, and in politics favors are not granted except on the basis of *quid pro quo*; the return that the newspaperman makes is to present the news as the politician wants it presented. But information regarding public affairs is public property. Sometimes it is not right to distribute it—as in the case of military secrets, for example—but even when it is not divulged it remains public property and the individual who happens to be entrusted with it cannot rightfully use it for his personal advantage. So when it is handed out to some favored newspaperman, the politician is giving, and the journalist is accepting something that belongs to neither, but to the public. It is not misappropriation in the legal sense, but in morals it bears a strong family likeness thereto.

Some eminent men have never seen this point. Theodore Roosevelt comes to mind at once, and Woodrow Wilson, the President who instituted the press conference, nevertheless sometimes resorted to the exclusive interview. Hoover used it consistently and toward the end of his first term Eisenhower seemed to be favoring it. Nevertheless, all these illustrious names cannot sanctify a practice full of the seeds of evil.

To end the digression and resume the thread of the argument: if the technical improvements in communication have enormously increased the speed of gathering news, they have also enormously increased its expense. As much may be said of the technical improvements in the printing trade; they produce marvelous results, but they require a tremendous capital investment and tremendous man power.

This is contrary to a widespread popular impression, namely, that labor-saving devices save labor in specific operations. They do not; they merely enlarge the operations. The fact that one linotype operator can do the work of many hand compositors doesn't mean that a modern newspaper can be produced with fewer printers because so much more type is required and there are so many more things to be done to it after it is set. I know of no prosperous newspaper that is being produced now with a smaller mechanical force than it employed thirty years ago.

All this entails the collection and expenditure of sums of money far beyond the reckoning of people unacquainted with the economics of the craft. A big-city newspaper—not meaning the *New York Times* or anything approaching its size, but a paper in any city of a million inhabitants—under modern conditions may easily cost $50,000 a day to produce. The bulk of that sum comes from local readers and advertisers, which is to say, it comes out of the business income of its city. Not many American cities can afford to pay more than $50,000 a day for news and only the very largest can afford to pay several times that sum. The result is that in most places the newspaper is as much a natural monopoly as the waterworks, or the telephone company. At present eighty-one per cent of American communities served by daily newspapers have only one, or have morning and evening editions under the same management. The tendency toward monopoly in the field of the daily press is an economic fact no less than the law of gravitation, and hardly more likely to be reversed.

This implies another condition. The management of a business employing anywhere from a few hundred to several thousand people and doing a volume of fifteen to twenty millions a year is a complex and difficult art that relatively few men can master. Newspaper publishing is big business at which none but a big businessman can succeed. But the mind of a big businessman is rarely the mind of a first-class journalist. The inquisitiveness, the skepticism of what is established and accepted, and the intellectual daring that are requisite to the discovery of truth under many wrappings of illusion are not qualities conspicuous in the managerial type.

This leads to the anomalous situation that newspapers— at least largely successful newspapers—are not controlled by newspapermen, but by industrialists. This imposes a limit on the newspapers' attainable professional excellence. If you select at random any one of the dozen biggest newspapers in the country, I dare assert without equivocation that it has, today, a staff capable of turning out a paper at least a hundred per cent better than the one it is producing; but I assert no less boldly that if the staff did produce such a newspaper it would go broke with great rapidity. It would sell, no doubt, but for nothing like what it would cost to produce. The dexterity of the industrialist in closing the gap between cost and selling price is essential to maintain the property; but that dexterity is inevitably damaging to the quality of the product.

This inescapable necessity has lain upon the press ever since the chief source of its revenues shifted from its readers to its advertisers; for readers and advertisers require of the press different and not entirely compatible services, the reader requiring information and the advertiser requiring display space. The demand for advertising space has led American editors into their most conspicuous professional fault, their tolerance of deft and beautifully machined but indubitable overwriting. The reporter who has no more to report than, "All quiet along the Potomac tonight," but who can say it in eight hundred words, is valuable because he fills a column and justifies the addition of a page to the paper, the other seven columns being sold to advertisers.

Some editors repudiate this furiously. They maintain that the great sorrow of their lives is the incorrigible tendency of reporters to pad their copy. They point out that they pay the copy desk enormous sums and supply it with unlimited blue pencils precisely for the purpose of cutting out the straw and sawdust before the copy goes to the composing room. True; but what the copy desk does is rip out the completely idiotic bunk, so unskillfully written as to be obvious and repulsive. The desk lays no unhallowed hand on the copy of the veteran who can write smoothly, gracefully, often almost brilliantly without conveying any information, or anything recognizable as an opinion.

To write beautifully and say nothing is so far from impossible that it may be described as an occupational disease of the craft of journalism. This fatal facility lies in wait for the veteran reporter as certainly as cirrhosis of the liver lies in wait for the addict to the gin bottle. It is encouraged by the city desk in that after every big news break it demands a long series of follow-up stories, frequently when there is nothing to report. If you have three hundred columns of advertising to balance with reading matter, reading matter must be had, and quantity takes priority over quality.

I mention this technical problem as illustrating one effect of journalism's rise—or fall—to the status of a great industry. But it is technical, therefore of interest chiefly to the professional. There are other effects of more immediate concern to the reader, and of larger social and political importance, that are also traceable to the dominance of the industrialist over the craftsman. These are the effects that worry such observers as Mr. Stevenson. That they are important is evident. That they are sinister may be plausibly argued. That they may become disastrous is not impossible. Hence they are more than newspaper problems, and should be understood by every American whose mind is influenced by journalism, which is to say, every man, woman and child in the country.

For reasons that will presently become apparent the writer insists on beginning this discussion with an opinion based on many years of study and comparison but, in the nature of the case, not demonstrable with the clarity of a proposition in Euclid. It is the opinion that as regards early, accurate and comprehensive factual information the American people today are better served than any other people in the world. It is possible that there may be an individual newspaper or two that in one respect or another is better than any newspaper existing in the United States; and many intelligent people regard the British Broadcasting Company's Third Programme as better than anything presented by American radio. But if you take in the whole picture, considering villages, towns, and small cities, as well as great centers of population, you will, I believe, find American journalism faster, more accurate, and more comprehensive than any other.

Yet it could be all that and still be poisonous. This is possible because the deadliest of all lies is a half-truth. If Americans are being served half-truths in enormous quantities, their minds are being poisoned more effectively than they could be by any other method. No candid student of public affairs will deny that the media of communication do serve up half-truths from time to time. Human fallibility makes that inevitable. The question, therefore, is one of relativity—to what extent and to what end is this done?

If one could answer, to a very small extent, and to no purpose at all, but simply by reason of the irreducible margin of error present in all human endeavor, then one might give American journalism a clean bill of health without argument. But a man must have small regard for his own reputation for candor if he makes any such claim after having spent thirty years as a member of the craft. Not all journalistic mistakes are honest mistakes, and it is silly to shut one's eyes to the fact.

The debatable point is not the existence of error, but the extent to which errors, honest and dishonest, are poisoning public opinion. To determine this is difficult, but not impossible, for it is a factual investigation. We have already a small library of studies of the press and radio, made by social scientists of every degree of competence from the masterly to the idiotic. The most notable is the so-called Hutchins Report which, although obviously inaccurate in some details, has stood up pretty well against vigorous assault; and the Hutchins Report was, on the whole, reassuring. On a smaller scale were several studies of press coverage of the presidential campaign of 1956; and all, including that made by the *New Republic*, certainly not biased in favor of the conservative press, were favorable. As of here and now the stream of factual information is not heavily polluted at the source.

What is far more difficult than measuring the existing situation is determining the direction and the rate of its changes. To employ a mathematical simile, measuring what exists today, however complicated, is still basically an arithmetical operation; but when you begin to handle the rate of change you can no longer rely on arithmetic, you have to proceed into the calculus, which is enough to strain the intellectual seams of the ablest operator.

To make even an informed guess at the situation that will exist ten years, or twenty years hence, you must balance the probable state of journalism against the probable state of public opinion at that time. For in this matter there is a process analogous to the medical process of immunization, and it must be taken into account. Mithradates Eupator, King of Pontus, is said to have preserved his life from assassins by taking progressively larger doses of toxic substances until, as Dumas remarked, he habitually breakfasted on a cup of poison, yet lived long and prospered. By analogy, consider Wilson's practice of "balancing lies," which may fairly be regarded as intellectual toxins. It has already been pointed out that the method is not unknown to the American newspaper reader and radio listener, and to the extent that he adapts and perfects it he develops immunity to the effects of bad journalism.

This is a factor rarely given much weight by sociologists, perhaps because it is elusive to a high degree, but the rate at which individual judgment is being suppressed and abolished by the tremendous lure of advertising has a decisive influence on any sort of prediction. It is not to be denied that Madison Avenue has refined the art of psychological appeal to a degree that might bewilder Dr. Rhine, with all his extrasensory perceptions. But it is certainly possible that here as elsewhere action and reaction are equal and opposite. If the skepticism of the customer increases *pari passu* with the skill of the advertising copywriter, there would seem to be no convincing reason to apprehend the early collapse of individual judgment.

There is as much plausibility in the theory advanced in an earlier chapter, that the lies told about one cigarette are counteracted and neutralized by the lies told about another; and so with washing machines, and automobiles, and television sets and all the other gadgetry whose profits go to the support of, among other people, journalists and even college professors. Advertising, by its very contentiousness, seems to have had the effect of making the American the most discriminating purchaser in the world. The evidence is not statistical. It is the increasing level of efficiency of all the things that are pressed upon the buying public in this country. "Soap opera" has come to be a term of derision in the American language, and it may be true that the superiority of one brand of soap over another is purely a figment of the copywriter's imagination; but it is the judgment of travelers that *any* American soap is better than the soap offered at an equivalent price anywhere else in the world.

It is highly significant that it was not always so. A look

at the advertising columns of, say, 1900, not in some wretched gutter sheet, but in the stateliest newspapers and magazines, will establish the point. The obvious swindles that grandfather fell for are almost beyond belief. It does not follow that we are the old gentleman's intellectual superiors; but it does seem that as sales prospects we are appreciably harder-boiled.

It would no doubt be fatuous to suggest that there is anything like a close parallel between the soap market and the market of ideas, but it would be equally fatuous to deny that there is a certain resemblance between them. Competition tends to eliminate the unfit in both; and that is the basic justification of freedom of speech and of the press.

It seems, therefore, that as far as preservation of American freedom is concerned, the factual accuracy of what is presented to the public by journalism is not conclusive. The fact that a lie is printed is not proof that the reader has been betrayed; if at the same time another lie is presented flatly contradicting the first, he may be only bewildered, in which case he may be stimulated to make an effort to find out the truth, and end by being educated. It is when only one lie is printed with no counteracting mendacity that the reader is definitely injured.

This is the appalling danger in journalistic monopoly. When only one newspaper or one radio station is available, it takes an almost superhuman sense of duty to restrain the proprietor from selecting from the news offered him, and especially from the opinion offered him, only such material as coincides with his own views, without including a fair representation of the opposing facts and opinion. It is not fair, and it certainly is not good public policy to rely upon the possession of a superhuman sense of duty by any group.

Radio and television are subject to one unavoidable restriction from which the press at present is free. Since the number of channels available is limited, allocation of channels by some central authority is the only means of avoiding complete chaos. We have entrusted this duty to the Federal Communications Commission which is, of necessity, a political body. The law has been drawn with great care to guard against the intrusion of politics in the operations of the FCC, but the ingenuity of man has never yet invented a law that will prevent a political body from being political. One might as well hope that by getting a court order changing MacGregor's name to Perkins, you can thereby prevent him thereafter from being a Scotchman.

By the same token, now that the daily press has become Big Business, it will display the psychology of Big Business. It is not a matter of volition, it is inevitable, and it is folly to attempt to attach moral turpitude to a historical process. The sensible course is to face the facts and adapt our attitudes and especially our habits of thought to them.

This is being done, has already been done, to a larger extent than many social scientists are willing to admit. The relative impotence of the press in politics is evidenced by the fact that in five successive presidential elections its advice was ignored by the voters, and in the sixth and seventh it was accepted only as regards the candidate for President, who happened to be a national hero. His immense popularity won Congress for his party by the thinnest of majorities in 1952, but at the first opportunity the voters reversed that decision, and in 1956 emphasized that reversal by increasing the President's majority and reducing that of his party to a minority. I do not see how, in the face of the facts, any rational man can escape the inference that the masses clearly understand that the press does not speak for them and its advice carries no more weight with them than does the advice of other segments of Big Business.

The lesson of the last seven elections is simply that the voting public is well aware that the official opinion of the newspaper is the opinion of the publisher, who is basically not a professional man, but an industrialist. His function in life is to apply labor to raw material and sell the resultant product at a profit. His opinion on politics is entitled to exactly the respect accorded the opinion of the president of a can factory or a textile mill, no less and no more.

Nevertheless, the publisher has yet another shot in his locker. If he can no longer sway public opinion by speaking, he may yet sway it very effectively by silence. This applies with especial force to communities in which not only the local newspaper but also the local radio outlet is controlled by one corporation. In such localities it is possible for one man to lower an Iron Curtain, shutting off not so much news as dissenting opinion. This is effective because men who could not easily be misled by misinformation can be trapped by lack of information as to what is being thought as well as what is being done in other places. This was realized a long time ago in this country. There is no doubt whatever that the Committees of Correspondence set up by the colonies had an important influence in bringing on the American Revolution, and many historians are convinced that it was a decisive influence. A community unaware of what other communities are thinking regarding problems common to them all is isolated in the very worst sense.

This raises a question that is already interesting farsighted men and that will probably become increasingly important within the next ten years. Economic trends have given an industrialist a monopoly position as regards the distribution of news and opinion in most cities—in eighty-one per cent, to be exact. The enormous costs involved make the newspaper a natural monopoly, and there is nothing that can be done about it. But it is long-established public policy that where natural monopolies exist they must be subject to public regulation.

The newspaper is a public utility in that a man cannot function effectively as a citizen of a democracy without accurate information. This means that to be a good citizen he must read a newspaper, just as certainly as that to be an efficient worker he must have a telephone. The question then is, to what extent should this monopolist be protected in the right to express his opinions on politics and attach them to an essential article that a man must receive into his house?

If the president of the telephone company used the back of the monthly bill, which everyone must receive, to argue the case of his political party, the howl that would go up would blow the roof off the city hall. But where there is only one newspaper, a man, to be informed, must receive it; so a very plausible argument can be made in favor of legal prohibition of publication of any opinion on politics by a newspaper holding a monopoly position in its town.

This brings us squarely up against the First Amendment, and some publishers are foolish enough to assume that that ends it. But that is far from ending it. The First Amendment, guaranteeing freedom of the press, gains its validity from the people's belief in the principle it embodies, and from nothing else. If the time should come when a majority, or even a considerable minority of the people should lose interest in sustaining it, the First Amendment would be of no more effect than the Eighteenth Amendment was after the public lost interest in making it work.

This possibility has been recently illuminated by Senator Eastland's thinly-disguised attack on the *New York Times*. The significant fact was not the attack but the languor of the protest against it. In 1955, Senator Eastland, ostensibly searching for Communists in journalism—although what business the Senator had with Communists engaged in private enterprise never has been explained—summoned some forty witnesses, three fourths of them men who worked, or had worked, for the *Times*. Every veteran newspaperman knows that there isn't a big newspaper in the country that hasn't had a Pink or two, or perhaps a genuine Red, working for it at one time or another. There should be at least one radical on every staff to give balance to the whole; so to give the impression that three fourths of them were concentrated on the *Times* was obviously an attack on that newspaper.

The animus of the politician needs no explanation. There never was a politician who has not now and then burned with desire to attack a newspaper, but in years gone by they rarely did it, and never without the strongest kind of proof, for it was exceedingly dangerous. The public was sensitive to a very high degree to any political assault on freedom of the press. But Eastland undertook it against one of the greatest newspapers in America and did it with relative impunity.

Never doubt that every other politician in the country took note. If the people are really losing interest in defending freedom of the press we may rest assured that very soon demagogues will be making a Roman holiday out of incinerating newspapers.

Freedom of the press never was intended to grant any special privilege to the printer. It was intended to safeguard the reader's freedom to read anything that is being said and thought on subjects that interest him. If the press no longer affords that freedom, then the reader's interest in protecting it is bound to subside; and if it subsides, then strength will inevitably drain out of the First Amendment.

As a newspaperman, I regard this possibility with unfeigned horror, and I am not at all convinced that the steps we are taking to prevent the catastrophe are intelligent. Certainly there is nothing intelligent in the tendency of some liberals to denounce the overlords of the press in unbridled language. My business happens to be of a kind that has brought me into contact with some dozens of newspaper proprietors whose properties range from country weeklies to some of the largest metropolitan dailies in the United States. Out of twenty or thirty individuals I can recall only two that I classify as outright rogues, and only three or four others whose most conspicuous characteristic was the possession of prehensile toes as well as fingers when a dollar was in sight.

For the rest, these men rank well above the average in general intelligence and at least as high as the average in honesty, fairness and generosity. All of them possess rather more boldness than the run-of-the-mine businessman; otherwise they would not be newspaper proprietors, for it is an extremely slippery form of property. Once in the red a newspaper can lose money faster than almost any other form of enterprise, crapshooting perhaps excepted, so timorous men do not stay long in the business.

The fatality of the situation is that the psychological pull is steadily against professional excellence of the highest kind. It is more than the fact that, as an investment, a mediocre newspaper is more profitable and very much safer than the best. It is also the fact that the very qualities that make the proprietor a good businessman tend to persuade him that a mediocre newspaper is in fact the best. This tendency is doubly strong in the field of reporting opinion, as opposed to that of factual events. The least conscientious publisher knows that to give a false report of an event, knowing it to be false, is scandalous; from which it is a short and easy step to the conviction that knowingly to permit any falsehood to appear in the paper is scandalous. Thus when the publisher encounters an opinion that he feels in the marrow of his bones is false, he bars it from his columns with a clear conscience.

Sound business is based on sound principles. The more completely honest your businessman, the more firmly he adheres to that axiom. It is correspondingly difficult for him to grasp the truth that the history of philosophy has demonstrated over and over that sound thinking is not necessarily based on sound premises. Opinion is in the realm of theory, in which the laws of the realm of fact do not necessarily apply. "The value of a doctrine in the history of science is not always commensurate with its degree of objective truth," says Gomperz in his history of thought. "A theory may be wholly true, and yet the unpreparedness of human understanding may make it useless and abortive, whereas a second theory, though wholly untrue, may render abundant service to the progress of knowledge precisely on account of that stage of intellectual development."*

He might have added that the soundest idea, if it is really novel, must by reason of its novelty seem untrue to the conventional mind. An illustration of this in our own political history may be found in the establishment of the Federal Reserve System in the first administration of Woodrow Wilson. Heaven knows, novelty could not be ascribed to that idea, which had been attacked and defended for generations. It was new only as regards its application to the American banking system; but even so, a long procession of the most eminent bankers in America paraded through Washington denouncing the system as impractical, leading inevitably to socialism, and utterly ruinous. A few of them may have been hypocrites, but the great majority were perfectly sincere; they were simply unable to adjust their thinking to ways which it was not accustomed to follow.

As far as a newspaper publisher is concerned the test of truth in this field is not, is this opinion true?, but merely, is it true that some honest and intelligent men hold this opinion? If the second question can be answered in the affirmative, then the duty of the newspaper to present the opinion is clear, unless it eschews the presentation of any opinion, including

* Gomperz, Theodor, *Greek Thinkers*, translated by L. Magnus, vol. i, 232.

its own, and confines itself to the role of a mere chronicler of events.

The lurking danger in this situation is the fact that any liberty that is not exercised tends to atrophy; and a great many American newspapers are not exercising their liberty to present all points of view. It is not necessary, however, to jump to the conclusion that the press is therefore permeated with evil. It may be due to nothing more blameworthy than a psychological lag. The thinking of newspaper proprietors has not kept pace with the change in their economic position. It is human nature whenever possible to accept privileges without assuming the accompanying responsibilities. Too many newspaper proprietors have become monopolists without recognizing their responsibility to become at the same time public servants, offering equal services to all comers.

In fairness it must be added, however, that a really astonishing number have done just that. All through the country you find scattered newspapers that, holding a monopoly, are nevertheless careful to present opinion flatly opposed to the newspaper's own policy. In many cases this opposing opinion is presented by famous syndicate writers more brilliant than anyone on the local staff, and accordingly more persuasive. This is rough medicine for the proprietor to take and he is due all the more honor for taking it. It means that he is putting his duty to the public above his own inclinations, which is always honorable.

But those who are subverting their duty are numerous enough to be building up a very sour public opinion regarding the theory of freedom of the press. This is perhaps no more than was to be expected, but it is none the less unfortunate for the rest of us because when public opinion goes sour it nearly always results in ill-advised action, frequently legislative action. The law is and has always been a very clumsy instrument with which to implement the Bill of Rights because the first eight amendments are all negative, forbidding intervention by the law. They are based on the supposition that there exists a positive demand for freedom. If there is no such demand the amendments are meaningless, and legislation based on an organic law without meaning is certain to be bad law.

So it works down to this—freedom of expression, which is inseparable from freedom of opinion, will inevitably disappear unless there is a strong and insistent demand for it; and there will be no strong and insistent public demand unless freedom of expression is obviously valuable to the public. A freedom that is enjoyed by nobody in town except one newspaper publisher is of small value to anybody else and will not be vigorously defended by the public. It is my belief that unless the great majority of those publishers who have attained a monopoly accept the responsibility that goes with monopoly there will be some form of political interference with freedom of the press within the next ten years.

My one reason for refusing to make that a flat prediction

is my belief in the increasing political competence of the average American. I know that there are observers at least as perceptive as I am who do not share that belief. Nevertheless, there is evidence, and to me it is conclusive, that the typical American voter is a more competent agent of self-government now than he was a generation ago. It may be that he is at, or approaching, a level of political education at which he will be able to value freedom in the abstract. When, as, and if that level is attained, he will defend freedom of the press even though it may seem to him that most of its benefits accrue to one big businessman.

It is to his interest to do so, of course, for as long as the principle remains intact some means will be discovered of applying it in practice. My guess is that this means will be found in an increasing number and variety of journals of opinion. It is true that their history to date has not been encouraging. The most intelligent ever produced on the conservative side, the old *Freeman* of Albert Jay Nock, lasted barely two years, and the chief survivors on the liberal side, the *Nation*, the *New Republic*, and the *Reporter*, never have been money-makers. But the conservative *U.S. News and World Report* seems to be doing very well despite the fact that the conservative point of view is well represented in the daily press.

The objections to all of these, liberal and conservative alike, are, first, that they are too slow, appearing weekly or bi-weekly; and, second, that their point of view is national, not local. The next generation, I believe, will see in all the larger cities of this country a multitude of small, cheaply-printed sheets published daily and devoted to comment and interpretation with a sharply local tinge. Then the typical citizen will read a newspaper to learn what is happening, but will turn to one of these small sheets to learn what it means from the conservative, or liberal, or other point of view. That is to say, the two functions of journalism, the dissemination of information and the dissemination of opinion, will be separated.

That is, however, mere speculation on a technical problem. It bears only indirectly on the fundamental issue, which is the question of preserving freedom of thought and expression in the face of increasing concentration of control of the media of communication. One way, of course, is to rely on the monopolist publisher to contine to exhibit a sense of duty to the public definitely stronger than the average, coupled with an estimate of the situation more realistic than the average. It is true that the conditions of his business stimulate both qualities in a publisher to a greater extent than they are stimulated in, say, a banker or a wholesale merchant. Nevertheless, the fact remains that the publisher who holds a monopoly position must exhibit a keener sense of civic responsibility than other businessmen, if the public is to be well served.

It has already been noted that in the conduct of public affairs it is both unfair and injudicious to base policy on the supposition that one particular group of citizens will rise above the general level, morally or intellectually. The most that may be reasonably expected is that no group shall fall far below it. To demand that newspaper publishers, as a class, maintain as high a level of integrity and intelligence as any other class of businessmen is no more than just; to demand that they exhibit a marked superiority in these respects is not just. Then to base public policy on the assumption that they are going to be superior is both unjust and unwise.

It is evident, then, that in the final analysis the survival of liberty depends far less upon the moral and intellectual quality of this group than upon progressive development of the political competence of the American citizen. Please note that this does not entail any such miracle as a measurable rise in either the moral or the intellectual rating of the mass of Americans. It refers only to an increase of their skill in the art of self-government. There is ample room for an increase of that skill without any change in their moral and intellectual status.

In point of fact it is nothing new to suppose that our political skill will increase as our experience lengthens. Far from being new, it is the original American political doctrine. The republic itself is a gamble, started in 1776 but still in progress, on the theory that the inhabitants of this continent were capable of learning an art that had never been thoroughly mastered in all human history, the difficult, slippery, ever-changing art of self-government by free men.

PERIL and PROMISE

Every day for a hundred and eighty years we have wrestled with this Proteus, and we haven't pinned down the old sea god yet. There has never been a moment without danger that self-government would elude our grasp and slip beyond control, but somehow we have contrived to hang on, and I have faith to believe that we are still capable of hanging on. Proteus constantly changes his shape into forms each more frightening than the last—from a Red Coat in 1776 to a Red Bonnet in 1800 to a Know-Nothing mob a little later, to Secession after that, to Prussianism, to Hitlerism, and now to Communism. But we still have him by the neck and no doubt he will presently change to something more frightful still. Nevertheless, we still have him by the neck, and not unless we grow tired and discouraged will he escape and overwhelm us.

II THE PROMISE

It is now almost exactly a hundred years since John Stuart
Mill remarked in his "Essay on Liberty" that one of the great
determinants of conduct has been "the servility of mankind
toward the supposed preferences of their temporal masters
or of their gods." It is, continued Mill, "not hypocrisy; it gives
rise to genuine sentiments of abhorrence; it made men burn
magicians and heretics."

The second part of this statement deserves more attention
than it has ever received from the average man, or probably
will ever receive while human nature is unchanged. It is hard
to believe that mere servility may be monstrous; yet the
central horror of the twentieth century is not its blood guilt,
but the fact that fiendish crimes could be tolerated by men
and women who were not hypocrites, but merely servile, accepting the word of diabolical leaders that these atrocities
were necessary.

This, not the bloodshed, has led some observers to believe
in an actual deterioration of human nature. Hear, for example,
the measured words of an eminent publisher:

PERIL and PROMISE

Despite many advances in social organization, despite the removal of many plague-spots from our national life, people, on the average, are nowadays more selfish, far more preoccupied with their own interests, far less interested in other people's concerns, than they ever were when I was a boy. When one pauses to look back for a moment over the history of the last thirty years, and when one observes what a widespread callousness, in face of everything that has been happening to our fellow human beings, has characterized it, one is appalled by the contrast. I think it was Leonard Woolf who wrote a brilliant article the other day, comparing the horrified protests that arose all over the world when, round about 1870, some unknown individual was kicked by a Prussian officer, or when a single Jew, Dreyfus, was the victim of injustice—comparing this with our relative indifference at a time when millions of human beings have been dying of starvation.*

As a matter of fact, Mr. Gollancz went too far back. It wasn't in 1870, it was as late as 1913 that the outrage perpetrated on "the cobbler of Zabern" infuriated the world. And the cobbler wasn't even killed; he was merely kicked aside because, being crippled, he couldn't get out of the way of a swaggering officer fast enough. Yet the incident created in this country a detestation of Prussian militarism that had a powerful effect in lining up American sympathies when the First World War started a year later.

A general deterioration of human nature is not, however, a necessary inference, even on this evidence. The inability of

* Victor Gollancz in *Personal Freedom*, a lecture delivered at Chelsea Town Hall and reissued as a supplement to *World Liberalism*, London, 1956.

an organism to respond to stimuli indefinitely repeated would seem to be enough to account for most of it. A veteran member of the homicide squad does not react to the sight of his twentieth murdered corpse as violently as he reacted to his first; but this does not necessarily imply that he is a worse man. The ordinary man of the twentieth century does not react to injustice to a single Jew as violently as he did before he had learned of the butchery of millions of Jews; nor to a beaten-up cripple as violently as he did before he had read of tens of millions of refugees kicked out of the way of advancing armies. Yet a man whose sensibilities have been dulled by repeated shocks may not be intrinsically a worse man.

What must be taken into account is the possibility that this erosion of emotional response may not account for all of the lethargy of the modern generation. In fact, we know full well that it does not. In part, it is due to the servility of which Mill spoke—the deference to the supposed preferences of some master, whether a contemporary *Fuehrer* or some venerated sage of the past.

A century after Mill wrote, this servility, while it may not actually burn heretics in this country, still makes some men join the Ku Klux Klan, some turn Catholic and others Protestant without any personal conviction, and converts some journalists into high-powered propagandists for causes that are as false as stairs of sand. But, as Mill observed, it is not hypocrisy; it is based on an utterly sincere belief that conformity is not only expedient, but also moral.

PERIL and PROMISE

One need not accept all the theories of the late Dr. Robert Lindner to realize that he touched an important truth in his protest against the acceptance of "the well-adjusted personality" as the psychological ideal. When we say "well-adjusted" all too often we mean a servile personality, which is an ideal fit only for a totalitarian state.

This trait in human nature is one secret of the success of the propagandist. It accounts for the power of the "snob appeal" in advertising as well as Fundamentalism in religion. The only successful defense against it is eternal vigilance against one's own tendency to accept servility as reasonable and right. Among Americans this danger is not great as directed toward a person because we have been indoctrinated against that kind of submission since 1776; but servility to a catch phrase is so common in this country as to be all but universal.

No prudent man will strike a holier-than-thou attitude in this matter. Liberal or conservative, wise or simple, naïve or sophisticated, we are all more or less vulnerable to catch phrases; the difference is that we are not all trapped by the same ones. The man who responds to "rugged individualism" is repelled by "the welfare state" and vice versa. In me, "free private enterprise" arouses suspicion; but I am aware that if you offer me any proposition under the guise of "freedom of speech" I am partially disarmed, laid open to suggestions of doubtful validity that would never catch me off guard if they were presented in other terms. So it is not for me to laugh when I see my neighbor bewitched by the magic words "national defense" into tolerating invasions of his personal liberty that a well-trained poodle ought to resent. To borrow a pet phrase of the Sage of Baltimore, I can only "cough sadly behind my hand."

This human tendency is familiar to every journalist who has reached the grade of master craftsman. Making skillful use of it is one secret of his trade, a means by which he can, if he is an honest man, do splendid work in promoting the general welfare. Unfortunately, if he is a crook the same means will enable him to perpetrate injuries limited only by by the height of his skill and the depth of his villainy. On the other hand, a reader who is keenly aware of this trait in his own nature is fortified against it and is usually a tough subject for the propagandist. Let us then examine the matter in some detail.

To begin with, there is no merit in the contention of some people, usually immature, that conformity is evil *per se*. But there is just as little merit in the assumption, especially common among ancient gaffers, that conformity is virtuous *per se*. Conformity is in itself neither good nor bad, it is completely neutral. Its one recommendation is that in many situations it is convenient. In an increasingly complex civilization human life is too short to permit a man to think through and form an independent, intelligent opinion on everything. For instance, there may be, for aught I know, logical reasons for the button-down collar on a shirt, and other logical reasons for using a clip. I have no opinion on the subject, nor do I expect to form one because life is too short to devote any of it to a subject of such slight importance.

There is no merit in non-comformity in matters of no importance. There is, in fact, demerit in it. The man who studies how to outrage the ordinary conventionalities is thereby convicted of spending his time and energy on trivialities, which is evidence that he is essentially a trivial fellow. The only occasion on which a man of sense refuses to conform to the fashion of the time is when fashion dictates something that is distinctly uncomfortable or otherwise annoying.

As it is with dress, so it is with the ordinary manners and customs of society. They may be senseless, but what of that? Any other set of manners and customs would be equally senseless, so why not conform to the set prevailing in the community? A man of genuine independence reserves his energy to do battle on things that really count; if one can devise no means of asserting independence other than going to a formal dinner in a plaid shirt, or attending an outdoor barbecue in white tie and tails, you may depend upon it that he is a shallow-minded faker. When it comes to a matter in which independence really counts for something, nine times out of ten you will find him falling in with the crowd.

Nor is the value of conformity, as an economizer of time and energy, confined to trivialities; there are many important affairs of state in which it is the only reasonable procedure for sensible men.

To take an extreme example, one that nobody will question, when it comes to the most advantageous deployment of the military forces of the United States it is utterly nonsensical for the civilian to attempt to form an opinion. This is a technical problem of great complexity, and what the Joint Chiefs of Staff say about it must be accepted by rational men, not because it is necessarily right, but because it is the best opinion available.

However, when it comes to the question of how much money we should spend on the armed forces, the situation is different. I doubt that the average man can form an intelligent opinion on the absolute sum, but he can certainly form one on the proportion of the total revenue of the government that should be devoted to armament. At present that proportion is tremendously high, and one of the chief problems of statecraft confronting the United States is how to reduce it without dangerously weakening national security.

This problem is technical only in part. There are two ways of assuring security. One is by strengthening defenses, the other is by reducing the threat. Defense is a military problem that must be left to military men. But in international relations the problem of reducing the threat is not military, it is political, and on politics the ordinary civilian voter has all the data that are available to general officers.

He may have more. If he has taken an active interest in politics ever since he reached voting age, he has had training and experience in the art of self-government superior to that of a man who has spent his whole adult life under military discipline, for men and officers in the services have little opportunity to learn politics at first hand. This is why the judgment of the ablest civilians on such matters as the portion of the national income to be appropriated for national defense is superior to that of the ablest professional soldier.

So it goes through all the problems that confront us as self-governing people. On technical matters of detail, conformity to the best expert opinion is essential, for the simple reason that the ordinary citizen has neither the time nor the facilities required to form an intelligent opinion of his own. At that, there is nothing particularly virtuous about it, except as the exercise of common sense is a virtue.

But the merit of conformity ends with its value in preventing waste of time and energy. It is regrettable that there is any excuse for making the statement. The average American ought to regard the assertion that there is no virtue in conformity as on a level with a solemn assurance that the sun really does rise in the east, never in the west.

Unfortunately, that is not the case. You can hardly pick up a newspaper without seeing an account of how some meeting was forbidden, or some speaker was refused a hearing on the ground that the topic to be discussed was "controversial." Only a few months ago a great deal of money was spent advertising the launching of a new magazine which its sponsors claimed would be different from any other periodical in the country, because it would carry nothing "controversial."

It is my considered opinion that in all the records of the fantastic there is nothing more ridiculous than the idea of a magazine worth reading that carries nothing controversial. It means, of course, that the magazine will contain nothing to provoke thought, for whatever provokes thought is of necessity open to question, that is, controversial. What you already know calls for no thought; it is the hitherto undiscovered truth that demands mental exercise, which is to say it is controversial by definition.

This effort to make "controversial" equal "infamous" has one, and only one sound reason behind it, which is, to make things easier for the police. If meanings are to be extended, let "police" be extended to cover a great deal more than the man in a blue uniform patrolling the streets; let it cover all regulators of conduct and expression, including the traffic officer under a cap, of course, but including also the Governor under a silk hat, the college president under a mortarboard, and the bishop under a miter. Let it include anybody who is considered and considers himself in any degree responsible for the maintenance of law and order.

Such authorities naturally deplore controversy, for controversy means that they must go into action, and going into action always means hard work and sometimes means risking defeat and humiliation. One should not attribute moral turpitude to them on this account. It is only human to dislike harassment and vexation. The official charged with the duty of sustaining any kind of orthodoxy would be more, or less, than human if he looked upon the heterodox with favor. Nevertheless, the growing tendency in this country to regard whatever is controversial as somehow immoral cannot inure to the benefit of anyone except the police. This holds good in every phase of life, beginning with the government itself.

This does not imply that the government is intrinsically or even relatively evil. It is the writer's firm conviction that democracy is the best form of government so far devised by the wit of man; but from this premise either of two equally valid inferences may be drawn. One is that democracy is good government; the other is that the wit of man is a feeble instrument. To my way of thinking, the fact that millions of Americans have drawn the first inference without even considering the second is one of the great weaknesses of democracy. Anything that is approved as nearly unanimously as democracy is approved in this country is in danger of growing stale; unless it is occasionally refreshed it begins to change its nature, very subtly perhaps, but very definitely. Sometimes unless the process is checked the approved idea turns into its opposite.

American democracy might well be stronger and better if it had vigorous and intelligent opposition. Unhappily, almost the only overt opposition it encounters is that of the Communists, whose theories are so obviously lunatic that it is impossible to get up a good argument over them. The thing that made my fellow townsman, the late H. L. Mencken, an exceptionally valuable citizen was his incessant, shrewd and well-aimed criticism of democracy, for which he would have substituted not Communism but aristocracy.

Many idolators of Jefferson completely ignore his repeated confessions of faith in the rule of the *aristoi,* the best, and his explicit assertion that "there is a natural aristocracy among men." Fond of quoting that line from the First Inaugural about reason being free to combat error, they are oblivious of the radicalism of the words immediately preceding it, words that flatly condemn the jailing of Secessionists or Communists, as long as they take it out in talk. If Jefferson could repeat that speech today, here is one opinion that he would add to it another purpose that such people can serve. This is the purpose of keeping democracy on its toes by stinging it out of the complacent lethargy into which any successful form of government is almost certain to drift.

Note well that Jefferson did not so much as intimate that nothing should be done about error of opinion. He assumed that reason would go into combat against it. He assumed that Americans would always regard controversy as a normal and wholesome exercise of the mental faculties. No more than John Milton could he "praise a fugitive and cloistered virtue, unexercised and unbreathed, that never sallies out and sees her adversary, but slinks out of the race where that immortal garland is to be run for, not without dust and heat." But both of these great protagonists of freedom were confident of the power of reason to overcome error without assistance from the arm of authority, legal or social.

Must we assume, then, that our present tendency to suppress non-conformist opinion lest it vanquish and destroy truth represents a degeneration that proves us unworthy sons of our great forefathers? I do not think so. I not only hope, I truly believe that our yielding to the terrors that beset us can be adequately accounted for on somewhat less melancholy grounds.

After all, why did Milton and Jefferson find it necessary to thunder so resoundingly? Obviously because the opposite opinion prevailed among a great many people in their day. Neither would have defended freedom of opinion had it not been threatened. So if it is appropriate in our day to echo their "hostility to every form of tyranny over the mind of man" the worst that can be said of our generation is that it has not advanced much in the centuries that have elapsed since the *Areopagitica* and the First Inaugural.

Still, that is bad enough. It is a sobering thought that today, even as when Mill wrote, a hundred years ago, and when Jefferson wrote, a hundred and fifty years ago, and when Milton wrote, three hundred years ago, the really terrible foe of liberty remains not any Caesar, or Sultan, or Great Khan, but the perennial, apparently indestructible "servility of mankind."

One reason why the thing is so startlingly apparent in these times quite evidently has no bearing on any change in the psychology—that is, the basic psychology—of the average American. It is the acceleration in the tempo of history. We have suddenly discovered that time is running out. We discovered it on August 6, 1945, the day that the atomic bomb burst over Hiroshima. On that day every American, whether he was a Piers Plowman in his furrow, or a Doctor of Philosophy in his library, discovered the truth of the grim motto popular for sundials: "It is later than you think." As a result, for more than ten years we have been a disconcerted people, and it is very difficult for disconcerted people to think calmly and logically.

We took note then of the tremendously important modification in Jefferson's statement. "Where reason is left free to combat it" error of opinion may be tolerated with safety. The plain inference is that if reason is not left free the whole proposition loses its validity. But reason does not act instantaneously. Its operations take time, and is there enough time left?

This is the great perplexity of our generation and it is the point at which human liberty is most seriously threatened. Wickedness and folly are the natural foes of freedom; we know that, and are not much disturbed by it, because it has always been so. Every advance in freedom since history began has been made against the frantic opposition of wickedness and folly and we expect nothing else. But when honesty and prudence seem to slacken in its defense it is another matter. When the Ku Klux and the Communists revolt against liberty, we feel more disgust than alarm. We expect nothing better of them. But when the Supreme Court of the United States deems it necessary to impose more and more restrictions on full freedom of expression, that is cause for anxiety.

For the Court does not take such action lightly. Justice Holmes explained its position with his dictum that freedom of speech does not include freedom to shout, "Fire!" in a crowded theater, thereby starting a panic. That isn't freedom, that is crime. By a long series of decisions beginning with the First World War the Court implied that to proclaim the right of revolution in America is now equivalent to shouting, "Fire!" in a crowded theater.*

The inescapable inference is that in the judgment of the Court the American people are more susceptible to panic than they were in earlier years. A member of the elder generation will hardly dare challenge this judgment. The elder generation has seen hysteria whipped up too often, from the Mitchell Palmer witch-hunt of 1919 to the McCarthyism of 1954.

* A series of decisions in 1957 suggests that the Court's anxiety on this score is abating.

70

THE PROMISE

Beyond peradventure most of this is attributable to the psychological shock administered by two great wars, with the attendant portentous advance in the destructive potential of modern science; but some of it is attributable to the development of virtually instantaneous communication. If this is not immediately obvious, a moment's thought will make it so. The destructiveness of an alarm in a theater is due to the fact that a thousand people receive the same shock in the same second; if the word spread gradually there would be no stampede. In 548, when the Emperor Justinian dismissed and disgraced his great general, Belisarius, the world was shocked, but by slow degrees. Before the news reached western Gaul the city of Constantinople was already adjusted to it. But fourteen centuries later, when King Hussein dismissed General Glubb, the jolt was felt in Paris, London, Washington and Tokyo within a matter of minutes.

This makes a difference, a very profound difference. It introduces into modern society an element of instability that lawmakers and judges must take into account, and that no thoughtful citizen can afford to ignore. And it brings journalism very prominently into the picture.

The media of communication, obviously, are not responsible for what, but only for how they communicate. They must transmit a true and complete account of events (with the stipulation that an important thought is as certainly an event as an important act). The impression that those events make upon the world and the response they draw are matters beyond the control of journalism. But he is a tyro indeed who does not understand that the total effect of what you say—at least when you are speaking English—is more than a little determined by the way you say it.

This is beautifully illustrated by the comment of a sardonic woman on a report from the twentieth reunion of her college class. One of her classmates was a certain Mary Jones, who was not only afflicted with an undue sense of her own importance, but whose taste in clothes ran to gaudy colors that clashed in a way beyond description and almost beyond imagination. Mary had missed several reunions and on her return she announced complacently that her presence at this one was the sensation of the day; whenever two class members met, she said, the first question was, "And have you seen Mary Jones?" Told this, the sardonic member commented, "True; but the way they said it was, 'Have you SEEN Mary Jones?' " Four simple English words, repeated four times in exactly the same order, will give you four different statements, if you stress heavily a different word in each repetition. Try it on this sentence: She only said no.

There is a parable for journalists here. It is not comforting; indeed, it is in many respects alarming, but it is apt. The explosive effect of any item of news can be appreciably increased or diminished by the way it is handled—by the placing of emphasis, by the selection of minor detail and, in the case of newspapers by its position and display.* This is, indeed, nothing new. It has always been known to competent news handlers. What is new is the total effect, for it increases in direct ratio to the speed of communication, which is now approaching the instantaneous.

In this modern world of lightning-fast communication and extremely jittery nerves it is hard to imagine a more serious offense against society than deliberately slanting the news to make it more terrifying than it need be. But there is one offense that is equally serious—it is willfully and knowingly to slant the news the other way, to make it seem reassuring when it is not reassuring. At a time when war, if it comes, will come faster than the speed of sound, crying peace, peace when there is no peace may lead to utter disaster.

The moral quality of irresponsible journalism, however, may be left for later discussion. What deserves emphasis at this point is certain prudential considerations that should serve as a checkrein on a hypothetical journalist with no morals at

* As this chapter was being written (February, 1957) the chief judge of the Supreme Bench of Baltimore city ordered a mistrial in a sensational murder case on account of an article and a photograph in the *News-Post*, a Baltimore evening newspaper. There was no question of the authenticity of the photograph and it was not taken in the courtroom. The court took judicial cognizance of the fact that the statements attributed to one of the prosecutor's staff had been accurately quoted and had been made in open court. Nevertheless, it was held that material factually accurate had been presented in such a way as to prejudice the defendant's case so seriously that a new trial was ordered. The ruling was in a court of original jurisdiction and might not be sustained by appellate courts; but it is at least suggestive of a disposition to hold the press to a stricter accountability than has been customary in the past.

all. These include a slow but sure loss of influence, which entails financial loss, by the newspaper, and an accompanying loss of status by the individual journalist. Eventually both lead to loss of freedom.

Advertisers, it seems to most working newspapermen, are as a class astonishingly slow to perceive their own true interests, but even advertisers have learned that circulation is not the only measure of value of a medium of publicity. The true measure is what is called "quality" circulation, which varies according to what the advertiser has to sell. It is utter waste to advertise your goods to people who cannot or will not buy them. There is no sense whatever in advertising beer in a penitentiary, or a new bond issue on Tobacco Road. Quality circulation is circulation among people who have the money and the taste to buy what you have to sell.

It is notoriously true that the extremely sensational press is a poor advertising medium for financial houses, bookstores and publishers, and the makers of fine and expensive products. What is often overlooked is the fact that the extremely sedate press is equally poor from the standpoint of such advertisers. Who ever thought of advertising mink coats and twenty-thousand-dollar automobiles in the religious press? There is no lack of confidence in the reliability of the church papers, but confidence alone is not enough. It is confidence in the paper by the right kind of readers, meaning, as a rule, readers with money, that turns mass circulation into quality circulation, thereby turning newspaper owners from millionaires into multi-millionaires.

However, this is primarily the concern of publishers. What concerns not only the publisher but also the craftsman, and most of all the reader, is the threat to freedom that irresponsible journalism entails. I said simply "freedom" not "freedom of the press," for the ramparts of liberty are continuous and a breach at one point threatens the whole citadel.

This is not only a danger, it is what the Supreme Court calls a "clear and present" danger. I know that many earnest souls are denying it, doubtless in all sincerity. Only a few months ago an important national magazine carried a long, labored and ingenious article the theme of which was that the American today has more, not less personal freedom than he ever had before. I have no doubt that the writer was reporting his own experience truthfully; but it appears that he is one of those people who have no desire to do anything not consistent with the existing climate of opinion in this country. If a man has no desire to do anything except what the Communist party wants done, he can be a perfectly free man in Russia; but it will hardly be argued that freedom flourishes in that country.

The only true liberty, in Acton's definition, is freedom to do what your conscience tells you is right. If your conscience has told you, in 1957, that every act of the Eisenhower administration was verbally inspired by God, then you may, indeed, have enjoyed in that year more freedom than ever fell to the lot of an American before. But as regards the country at large, that is not the test. The test is that other fellow's freedom, the one who, in your opinion, is a low-lived, iron-skulled, leather-lunged donkey—is he free to do what he wants to do, short of infringing upon your rights or violating the criminal law? If he isn't, then your feeling of perfect liberty is illusory; what you are enjoying is not freedom, but only "the servility of mankind" that would enable you to live at ease in a slave state.

Here is the point, stated in more decorous and more beautiful language than I can command: "We should be eternally vigilant against attempts to check the expression of opinions that we loathe and believe fraught with death." That is Mr. Justice Holmes, speaking in the Abrams case, and uttering the most powerful argument for freedom of opinion that has been put before the country within memory of living men. Holmes was one of the most learned men in the United States, but he said, "Every year if not every day we have to wager our salvation on some prophecy based upon imperfect knowledge." It follows that the very opinion we loathe and believe fraught with death may contain the more perfect knowledge that would effect our salvation.

Yet even Holmes had to admit a qualification. Immediately after the words quoted above he conceded that sometimes expressions of wrong opinions may "so imminently threaten immediate interference with the lawful and pressing purposes of the law that an immediate check is required to save the country."

There is the loophole through which tyranny may yet creep in to seize the stronghold of liberty. The gap is disturbing the best minds in the country; it has produced a whole shelf of books within the past year or two from men as diverse in temperament and outlook as Reinhold Niebuhr and Elmer Davis; but nobody has as yet devised a means of closing it without precipitating worse evils. Perhaps nobody ever will, for there are some questions that have no answers and this may be one of them.

But a gap that cannot be closed must be guarded, and the slight reliance of thoughtful observers on a free press as the effective bulwark of liberty is no slight embarrassment to newspapermen. Gone is the fine confidence of the republic's early days, the spirit that moved Jefferson to prefer newspapers without a government to a government without newspapers. The pressure of self-interest is presumed to be too powerful to resist, and the theorists look for their Horatius Cocles anywhere but in the ranks of the Fourth Estate.

Yet it has just been pointed out that in at least two directions the pressure of self-interest in modern journalism is not contrary to the public interest. This applies to the owner and to the wage earner, to the publisher and to the greenest cub reporter.

From the standpoint of the publisher, the most valuable of his commercial assets is public confidence. A widespread belief that his newspaper is not telling the truth, or not telling the whole truth, may not materially reduce his total circulation, if he holds a monopoly position, but it does cut sharply into his quality circulation. When it becomes a matter of common knowledge that the most intelligent and influential citizens in a community have to buy, and do buy an out-of-town newspaper to make sure that they are adequately informed, the value of the local publisher's property is definitely impaired. His high-class advertising, which is his highly profitable advertising, tends to dwindle or to slip away because it is not as productive to the advertiser. The loss to the newspaper in such a case is not measured entirely by the loss of linage, because it is the high-priced linage that is going; and this is a leakage that no newspaper property can stand indefinitely.

From the standpoint of the hired hands, rather than the publisher, a gradual loss of public confidence in the paper means to the working journalists who actually write it a gradual loss of professional status which is pretty sure to be attended by loss of earning capacity. Few laymen understand to what an important extent a newspaperman's standing in the craft is affected by the reputation of the journal for which he works. Leg men may not be much affected, but after a man has reached stardom the fact that he has worked for certain newspapers is no recommendation when he is applying for a better job; managing editors of many of the best newspapers in the country have an inviolable rule against hiring a man who is known to have worked for a disreputable sheet, and are reluctant to take on one from a paper that may be respectable, but is notoriously biassed.

That is to say, the publisher's financial interest and the news writer's professional interest are both impaired by loss of public confidence in the reliability of the journal. This is not glaringly obvious; some degree of shrewdness is necessary to perceive it, so it is not much of a deterrent as far as the stupid are concerned. But in this business the stupid do not survive long anyhow, and it is a deterrent to the intelligent. When journalism gets too bad it cuts its own throat.

Pray remember, though, that this describes the situation of the hypothetical journalist with no morals at all, an inert object moved entirely by outside forces. In his case servility, which is a weakness, pulls him toward abandonment of freedom; but self-interest, another weakness, pulls him the other way. If he is governed by his weaknesses alone he tends to be, like Mahomet's coffin, suspended in midair. However, the journalist with no morals at all is strictly hypothetical; no man ever lived without some inner drive, some impulse generated within, not received from without, and this temperament is always important and may be the decisive influence in a man's career. Attention will be paid to that in another chapter.

But before abandoning the hypothetical inert object there is a *tertium quid* that must not be ignored. If servility pulls the journalist one way and self-interest another, there is a third force that operates on him with great power. This is public opinion as it exists in his immediate neighborhood, and the direction in which it drives him varies with the locality—or, perhaps one should say, with the level of civilization in the particular locality.

Sentimentalists are loath to admit it, and politicians raucously deny it, but the fact is that we have in this republic certain communities in which the level of civic virtue and general intelligence is so low that it is flatly impossible to produce a decent newspaper in such hog wallows. These are not necessarily the forlorn, starveling sinkholes described in *Tobacco Road*; in some of them the acquisitive instinct has worked so powerfully that the denizens have amassed large quantities of money and live in gaudy luxury as far as material possessions are concerned. Their pauperism extends only to things of the mind and spirit.

The relatively civilized remainder of the country lives, for the most part, unaware of these foci of moral infection until some startling incident draws attention to them—a race riot, a lynching, or, more often, the savage persecution of some luckless wight who has been incautious enough to tell the truth. Then our eyes are opened to the embarrassing blots on the 'scutcheon—the ease with which everything admirable in American life may be burlesqued and turned into obscene farce, commerce being turned into organized swindling, industry into slave-driving, religion into fanaticism, and patriotism into a Dionysiac orgy of horrible old women, screaming maenads who fall upon intelligence and rend it, as the Bacchae rent Orpheus limb from limb.

Investigation of the history of one of these plague spots almost always reveals that ignorant and incompetent journalism contributed heavily to its degradation; but so did ignorant and incompetent commercialism, theology and jurisprudence. The end product is a community in which it is impossible for intelligent journalism to survive; but it is, if not the rule, yet often the case that the climate of opinion is equally unfavorable to an enlightened business policy, to the administration of justice, and to the development of any spiritual religion, Christian, Judaic or Islamic. In brief, all civilization declines.

But let us stick to our muttons, leaving the merchants, the parsons and the politicians to look after their own. The dark forces of ignorance and prejudice that make honest journalism impossible in some communities exist in all communities and always tend to degrade the media of communication. Yet wherever civilization consists of something more than a silk hat and tail coat put upon a Hottentot with neither trousers nor shoes, public opinion furnishes counter-agents that brace up journalism faster than barbarism can tear it down.

This is the third force operating upon the journalist regardless of his wishes, and it is by long odds the most powerful of exterior pressures. Granting that public opinion is impotent against the really strong personality, it can nevertheless work wondrous transformations in the weak and the mediocre, the classes to which most of us belong. Public opinion can never convert Lion-Heart into a mouse, but it can and it constantly does convert a mouse into Lion-Heart, at least for the moment.

This is why it is fairly safe to assume the existence of a highly civilized community wherever you find a highly civilized newspaper. The rule is not absolute. Occasionally some figure of heroic stature appears in an unfavorable environment and survives there for a time; *per contra*, occasionally a scavenger sheet will appear briefly in a respectable community. Such exceptions produce drama, which may culminate in tragedy, such as the assassination of Don Mellett, in Canton, Ohio, thirty years ago, or in triumph, such as the achievement of William Rockhill Nelson in Kansas City. But it is inevitably transient. When a good newspaper appears in a barbarous town, one of two changes is certain within a few years—the town will become better, or the newspaper will become worse.

To advance toward an estimate of the total situation, then, it is necessary first to make an estimate of the net effect of the climate of opinion on the American press. It may operate, in fact does operate, in opposite directions—here as a drag, there as a stimulant. In the absence of any means of statistical measurement, whatever judgment is rendered on this point must be no oracle but merely an opinion which is, at best, no more than an informed guess.

Yet opinion in this case may rest on bases that are not guesses, but historical facts. One of the most interesting of these is the fact that the American people, while as likely to develop emotional crises as any other population, have demonstrated for nearly two hundred years an astonishing power of recuperation; and the recovery, as a rule, is sudden and inexplicable.

Consider—to mention only a few of the more spectacular delusions that have threatened personal liberty—the Alien and Sedition laws, Know-Nothingism, Anti-Masonry, the Mitchell Palmer Red Scare, Ku Kluxism and McCarthyism. In each case after going far, sometimes dreadfully far, along the road to lunacy, we have suddenly pulled up. In none of these cases were we saved by the intervention of some hero; in most of the cases heroes who fought the menace were conspicuously lacking among politicians, and most numerous, yet all too few, in the press. What did the work seems to have been an unexplained revival of common sense among the masses of the people. All at once the typical American decided that the whole thing was a bore, and refused to get excited about it any longer.

It distresses moralists and logicians to suggest that great political issues are subject to decision by whims as unpredictable as the fad for Davy Crockett suits, but the evidence is plain. Nor is it entirely discouraging. It implies the existence of a vast reserve of sanity among the common people, a reserve large enough, if it can be brought into action, to beat down all the Lords of Misrule that have threatened us in the past.

The qualification, "if it can be brought into action," is, of course, immensely important. There is always the possibility that one of these fits of hysteria may carry us to the point of no return, beyond which lost liberties can never be regained. But it hasn't happened yet. To date, the appeal to reason has always succeeded before the damage was beyond remedy.

One has factual evidence then that since 1789, when the Constitution went into effect, the idiocy of American democracy, incontestably present, has, on the whole, been outweighed by the wisdom of democracy, also incontestable. If it be granted that the function of the journalist, ideally, is to promulgate wisdom, and if it be admitted that his functioning is conditioned in part by his own weaknesses and in part by the pressure of public opinion, then his case is not hopeless by a long Scots mile. For his two chief weaknesses, servility and selfishness, tend to neutralize each other, and the third compulsion, public opinion, drives him oftener to the support of freedom than to its betrayal.

Surely it is needless to emphasize the importance, both to journalism and to society, of omitting no effort to stimulate the development of a healthy public opinion and to combat its opposite. But that is the duty and interest of every self-respecting citizen, not that of journalists alone or chiefly.

Based on these grounds the opinion is herewith advanced

that the conditions under which the American journalist works at the present time offer a promise as well as a peril to free-men who are resolved to remain free. But it would be to strip them of their manhood to assert that the conditions undei which they work are the sole determinants of the conduct of members of the craft. After the conditions have all been taken into account, and after an effort has been made to give to each its due weight, there remains the man himself, meaning the complex of temperamental qualifications requisite to en-able an individual to practice this craft successfully.

If the mental and emotional qualities that go to make a first-rate newspaperman go also to make a robot, then the chances are even that a robot he will be, regardless of the conditions under which he works; and in that case Adlai Stevenson's apprehensions are entirely justified. But if their tendency is strongly in the opposite direction, then you can load the newsman with more chains than Epictetus wore but you will not reduce his mind to slavery and, like the old philosopher, he will remain freer than his master and a dis-penser of freedom to others. Let us turn, then, to an examina-tion of these personal qualities.

III THE PERSONNEL

Diodorus Cronus, the Megarian philosopher, named one of his slaves Indeed, and another one But, as a protest against the tyranny of language. When the conventional were shocked, Diodorus argued—to state his case in modern terms—that there is nothing in law or in morals that restricted him to Tom, Dick and Harry, or, in the case of slaves, to Remus and Scipio as names. Tom, Dick, Harry, Remus and Scipio are all words. So are Indeed and But. Why, then, must we use one word rather than another to designate a human being?

Diodorus thus anticipated by some twenty-two centuries the argument of Humpty Dumpty to Alice in Wonderland that he had a right to make words mean whatever he chose to have them mean. Diodorus and Humpty Dumpty were conscious rebels, applying the Conventional Theory of language; but equally odd effects can be achieved by one who is not rebellious, but merely unwary, as witness the Aframerican who named his hound Moreover, and insisted that the name was Biblical, citing the account of the beggar Lazarus in Luke 16:21: "Moreover the dogs came and licked his sores."

THE PERSONNEL

Laugh if you please, but these absurdities reflect a very real difficulty of the journalist who regards his occupation as something more than the means by which he pays the rent on his house. He is the prisoner of language and he cannot share Diodorus' happy delusion that he can escape by defying it. Every practitioner of the craft runs into the bars whenever he has anything to report more complicated than the dullest routine; for to put into words exactly what you want to say, all that you want to say, and no more than you want to say is a triumph of literary art on a very high level, although the subject of the discourse may be nothing more important than a police raid on some honky-tonk in which the merriment was getting out of hand.

Literary triumphs are not achieved every day, not by a Homer or a Vergil, to say nothing of a rank-and-file member of the Newspaper Guild, slenderly equipped with brains and untouched by the divine afflatus. Yet the news writer must attempt it five times a week, and in cases of emergency seven. Naturally he is a frustrated man, and this is the first item to be taken into account in assessing his psychological equipment.

Frustration, as every amateur psychologist knows, is conducive to every kind of antisocial activity, from attempts at wife beating to attempts at overthrowing the government. What amateurs seldom know, although every professional does, is that frustration does not always drive men in the same direction; its effects are modified by what, when he started, the failure hoped and expected to accomplish. If the undertaking is notoriously one in which perfect success is beyond human capacity, failure to achieve it is not bitterly disappointing. This applies to all the arts, and to the crafts in measure as they rise above mere competence and approach art. The perfect picture has never been painted, the perfect poem never written, the perfect statue never carved. No more has the perfect news story ever appeared in print. But men do not on that account give over the attempt. Indeed, it is precisely in those lines of endeavor in which they know that they are beaten from the start that their most magnificent efforts have been put forth and their most remarkable triumphs won.

Hence to say that the journalist is a frustrated man does not carry the connotation that he is an enfeebled and embittered man, one with a tendency to join the Communist party, or to commit suicide by slapping his wife. Only in a minority of cases does the frustration of the journalist terminate either in melancholia or in genuine cynicism; a far more common result is a mild skepticism touching ultimate goals. Aware that in his own case the only attainable values are to be found in the effort, because the goal is beyond reach, he is tolerant of other men's failures and inclines to attribute to them much credit for a good try, regardless of the ultimate defeat.

However, in some cases, fortunately rare, it must be admitted that frustration does produce the absolute cynic, and a journalist who has gone that far is as dangerous a member of society as exists anywhere. We have then, on the level of the hired hands, such individuals as the Chicage *Tribune* reporter who was assigned to cover crime but, after some of his accomplices had shot him down, was found to have been master-minding crime; and we have, on the level of ownership, a James Gordon Bennett the elder, and a William Randolph Hearst.

Some people would list the vociferous McCormick, of Chicago, in this category, but it is questionable that he belongs there. The complete cynic believes in nothing, but there was one thing in which the Colonel did believe with all his heart, and all his mind, and all his soul, and all his strength. That thing was Robert R. McCormick. Bennett never believed in Bennett, nor Hearst in Hearst, and by so much their perfection as types exceeded McCormick's.

The thoroughgoing cynic is so unusual, however, that he may be disregarded in any attempt to estimate journalism as a social force. As regards the problem of political liberty, the mass of its practitioners are skeptics only, and rather gentle skeptics, at that. They have been taught that the freedom of the individual is the foundation of the American way of life. They observe that a great many individuals enjoy no real freedom, and that no individual is, or can be, perfectly free. But few of them are thereby driven to deny either the existence or the value of the concept of freedom.

The conditions of their own work forbid that denial. If perfect freedom does not exist, neither does the perfect news story; but that does not affect the existence of the concept of perfection. In their professional work—although not necessarily in other relations—newspapermen are Platonists. Imprisoned in language, like Plato's characters chained in the cave, they nevertheless believe that the shadow shapes on the wall before them relate to some reality in a larger world.

To carry over this idea from the field of professional technicalities into the larger field of public affairs is an easy psychological transition. To the extent that this transition is made, which is probably to a very large extent, the journalist is predisposed by the conditions of his daily labor to harbor a belief in the existence of political liberty as an ideal, and to attribute its relative scarcity in the existent world to inhibitions that, in theory at least, may be removed.

This leads to the odd conclusion that the very imprisonment of the journalist within the strong walls of language tends to strengthen his faith in the concept of freedom. But is it really strange? Who has a keener appreciation of the reality of liberty than the convict in a penitentiary? By the same token, a man whose daily task is to struggle with the difficulties of communication may be expected to have an uncommon appreciation of the value of free and exactly accurate communication, even though he may be skeptical of the possibility of ever attaining it.

It would seem, therefore, that the first characteristic of the working journalist tends to make him a supporter of the ideal of freedom of expression, rather than an advocate of restriction.

THE PERSONNEL

In the second place the journalist, being human, enjoys the exercise of power as much as a bishop, a judge, a Congressman, or a business tycoon enjoys it. Members of the craft are given to denying this, vigorously and often profanely. There is an old and honored tradition among them that any newspaperman who seeks power for himself, especially political power, is thereafter forever ruined as a newspaperman.

But there is no necessary conflict between these ideas. Long experience does, indeed, sustain the belief that a journalist who goes into politics suffers serious and permanent damage as a journalist. It does not follow, however, that this must be regarded as the penalty for his grasping at power; it may be merely that he sought it in a way inconsistent with his proper functioning as a journalist.

As a matter of historical fact most really great journalists have been in politics up to their necks throughout their active careers, and until the invention of the electric telegraph journalism was justly regarded as an appendage of politics. Fenno and Freneau were in fact politicians detailed to serve on newspapers, much as an artilleryman is first a soldier, and secondarily one detailed to use great guns instead of a rifle. Benjamin Franklin Bache was, perhaps, an exception, apparently having inherited his grandfather's taste for making printer's ink something more than a party implement; but not until much later did the newspaper itself become a reliable means of support for an able man. Thomas Ritchie, Duff Green, Amos Kendall and the original Francis P. Blair were none of them primarily newspapermen. They supported their newspapers by their political genius instead of relying on their journalistic ability for their political power. At that, none of them held any but relatively minor offices, usually by appointment, rather than by election.

Not until a good portrait painter wasted his time and ruined his art by inventing the electric telegraph did the gathering and dissemination of news become an occupation sufficiently rewarding to be a full-time job for a first-rate man. But with the coming of the telegraph the business became profitable enough to compete with commerce, industry, and the professions for high ability, and immediately practice of the craft became incompatible with office seeking.

Ever since, the really great success of the journalist in politics has been in the role of Warwick, the Kingmaker. Greeley, Dana, Bennett, the second Samuel Bowles, Medill, Hearst and Pulitzer were certainly political powers of the first rank as long as they abstained from personal participation; but when they violated that rule the results were usually disastrous. Dana's effort to force a political appointee on Cleveland started the quarrel that did most damage to his career. Greeley ran for President, and it killed him. Hearst's every bid for high political office ended in humiliating defeat. It is significant that the man who, from the strictly professional standpoint, may be regarded as the most successful of them all in that he created a great and long-lasting institution, regarded any personal appearance on the political stage with violent distaste. This was Ochs of the *Times*. On the other hand, the newspaper editor who rose higher in politics than any other was Warren G. Harding, a bad journalist and widely regarded as the worst President since Grant.

The power that the journalist may legitimately seek and may exercise without professional damage or psychological strain is the power of the printed word. It should be enough to satisfy the most ambitious, for it can be very formidable indeed. If we accept the common belief that the other great powers operative in this country are the political, the legal and the financial, then it can be plausibly argued that the power of the media of communication is second in the list, coming next after the power of money, and definitely ahead of that of the judge or of the public official.

The reason that some journalists do not see this is that, being human, they experience the common human difficulty in discerning the true nature of power. Vanity is blind; it cannot distinguish power from its trappings; and journalists have their full share of human vanity. A judge's robe, an officeholder's title, a tycoon's flunkies, catch the eye and confuse the thinking of a member of the craft as readily as they do the same thing for a shoe clerk, a schoolteacher, or a farmer.

It is an exceptional mind that in its early days, before it has been battered by years of experience, can grasp the truth that genuine power is simply the ability to produce a lasting effect. To achieve it is a laudable ambition. We pass this way but once, and a man is of little worth if he does not cherish some hope that after he has passed things will not be exactly as they were before. The centurion having authority may say to one, Go, and he goeth, and to another, Come, and he cometh. But the power is not his own; it is derived from the eagles and delegated to him only for the term of his command. Eventually he must hand it over to a successor, and he may vanish like the king in the Arabian Nights, whose bitter obituary was, "He died; and time passed over him, and it was as if he had never been."

Philosophy assures us, of course, that this is the ultimate fate of all. Let enough years go by, and the mightiest heroes of today will join the *fortes ante Agamemnona,* unless by a chance over which they have no control they shall happen to be embalmed in Homeric poetry. But we are here concerned not with philosophic speculation, but with the practical conduct of life; and as a practical matter we know that there are among us men who will not be forgotten at least until their last contemporary draws his last breath. To be numbered among them is an honorable aspiration for any man, a journalist as well as another.

Naturally, if a man cherishes a strong desire to amount to something more than a statistic in the census report he finds it to his interest to keep the way open to that goal. If the journalist's legitimate avenue is the power of words, he favors the maintenance and extension of that power for the same reason that the banker favors sound money, and the industrialist sanctity of contract. Banking becomes a nightmare when inflation of the currency runs wild, and manu-facturing would be impossible if no contract would hold. So, where freedom of speech is suppressed, journalism is not an art, a profession, or even a genuine handicraft; it is merely an exploded theory.

In Soviet Russia some men—Ilya Ehrenburg, for a con-spicuous example—have achieved luxurious living and wide-spread notoriety by writing for newspapers, but that they are practicing journalism will not be admitted by master crafts-men in this country. If you insist on being strictly technical, yes. Technically, the cub who is assigned to collect the names of eminent guests at the season's fanciest wedding is practicing journalism. By the same token, Ehrenburg, assigned to set forth his masters' ideas in language more graceful than the masters can command is in journalism; but he is paid an enormous salary for the same reason that a circus manager is willing to pay a high price for the best-trained poodle in the world.

In this country, too, we have trained poodles and they sometimes command salaries comparable to Ehrenburg's for the same kind of service—to jump through the hoop, to walk a tight wire, to roll over and play dead at the snap of the ringmaster's fingers. Their incomes are immense, their names are household words, and some of them cheat the gallows for many years, but they need not concern us here. This discourse applies to human beings only.

Without doubt there are thousands of newspapermen who

have never had the time or the inclination to pause and think
the matter through, but there is hardly one who does not feel
that freedom of expression, which in his case means freedom
of the press, has for him an interest that is not limited to his
professional status. His status is important, certainly; but if
it were not involved, still he would feel that any restriction
of his right to tell the truth as he sees it deprives him of something that he needs and values. Even when the right is not
questioned but the opportunity is denied, he suffers a feeling
of deprivation and tends to share the sour melancholy of the
eunuchoid.

So in the case of the journalist two legitimate aspirations,
the desire to enjoy the largest liberty consistent with the human
condition, and the desire to exert power, coincide to make him
a natural defender of free speech. But that is not all. Certain
traits that seem to be characteristic, not of every man but of
the successful journalist, take the same direction, and their
influence may be even more powerful than the two that have
been mentioned.

One of the best and wisest men that it has been my privilege
to know, a man whose eminence in scholarship had made him
head of his department in a great university, dumbfounded
me some years ago by remarking, "Sometimes I envy you,
who have remained in the world of action, instead of re-
tiring, as I did, into the academic cloister."

It was a demonstration of the curious ignorance of the

learned, for if there is anyone who is emphatically not a man of action it is the newspaper employee who works in the editorial, not the business end. His is the temperament of the born spectator, the looker-on, the perpetual sidewalk superintendent. His arch-fear is the fear of missing something, and he knows that the actors on the world's stage, especially the leading actors, miss a great deal of the by-play that is plain to the rejoicing galleries. His place is in the audience, his function to hiss and to applaud, to cheer and to jeer, and his happiness is to estimate the value of the performance for the benefit of those who may have had a less advantageous seat.

At first glance this may seem to be a contradiction of the preceding section which conceded to the newspaperman his full share of the human love of power. But a second glance will correct that impression. Ask an actor if he regards the audience as powerless, and he will shrivel you with a look. And among the spectators the leader of the claque is the man most to be feared and placated.

The antithesis of the man of action is not the paralytic, but the man of thought. There is no distinction between them as regards work. Indeed, there are few more laborious ways of making a living than journalism, taken seriously. The by-laws of the Newspaper Guild notwithstanding, a top-flight newspaperman, like an artist, or a scholar, works a hundred-and-forty-eight-hour week, for his work frequently invades his dreams.

PERIL and PROMISE

A reporter strolling in the park with his wife on his Sunday afternoon off duty, who happened to see it all when some hophead shot the Mayor, and who didn't instantly race for a telephone, would be—well, he would be unimaginable. Ask the wife. The not-by-any-means-secret sorrow of the ill-advised girls who marry newspapermen is precisely that experience, constantly repeated, of being left standing on the pavement to get home the best way they can, because some sudden event has sent their husbands haring off after the story. The wiser ones understand it, and tolerate it, but it is doubtful that any woman ever forgave it.

Yet the divorce rate in the craft is not conspicuously higher than it is in other occupations. Probably the reason is that the hardships and exasperations that attend the life, for wives as well as husbands, are in part compensated by the fact that it isn't a monotonous mode of existence. The wife's days are filled with deprivation, humiliation and indignation, but not with tedium; and it is astonishing how much can be endured by one who may be constantly outraged, but is never bored.

It is certainly true of the veteran journalist that he can stand anything better than dull routine. This is what has held him for years and decades to a craft that is laborious, nerve-racking and not highly remunerative. The boys who can take monotony usually get out after a few years and go into business, politics or the professions; it is those who must be entertained who stay to become the patriarchs of the news room.

That world-champion scorner, George Bernard Shaw, saw in this proof of the incorrigible immaturity of the trade. His definition of the journalist was a man born without the capacity to achieve accuracy in anything. Forgoing the obvious comment on the beauty of this as a self-portrait, let us admit its literal truth; the journalist does nothing quite right because he always attempts the impossible, to wit, perfect communication, which even the Apostle expected to attain only in that other world where "I shall know even as also I am known."

That has no bearing, however, on one's attitude toward freedom of expression, so far as that attitude is determined by temperament. Obviously, the born spectator wishes to see the show go on, and the greater the variety of the acts and the more eloquent the actors, the more complete is his satisfaction. To the reporter the saddest words of tongue or pen are "No comment." They mean that he has to fake the story, which is not only hard work, but inevitably bad work.

For this reason the journalist is temperamentally a vigorous advocate of free speech, for himself but even more for others. Censorship limits his satisfactions and impedes his efforts. He would be more—or less—than human if he were not violently against it.

Critics of the press decry this trait as in reality a desire not for free but for loose speech, the fuel of sensationalism. The criticism is not without factual basis, but it applies only to second-rate craftsmen, the immature or the irresponsible. It is doubtful that there is a single reporter of as much as

twenty years' experience who has not at some time cautioned
a friend in some such terms as, "Senator, I know what you
mean, but the way you have just said it is going to look like
hell in print." That isn't killing a story, that is preserving
a contact that may be invaluable in the future; for the Senator,
assured that the reporter's object is to learn the facts, not to
trap him in an incautious utterance, will talk all the more
readily.

Delight in mere novelty doubtless is childish, but a pas-
sionate wish to extend one's experience of men and things is
not. Possibly it is ingenuous. Possibly they are right who
maintain that an extension of experience is only an extension
of grief; but whether or not they are right, of one thing I am
fully persuaded—they are old. When a man has come to
the point at which he can no longer believe that there is anything worth seeing around the next corner he is old, and
whether his years be nineteen or ninety is irrelevant. But he
who is always hopeful that there may be a wonder to be seen
in the cross street will somehow make it to the corner, tottering
and gasping, perhaps, but getting there. And he may be old
in years and sin, but not in spirit.

During the late war a celebrated editor, then in his
seventies, was on a ship that was torpedoed in the North
Atlantic one winter's night. Taken off in a lifeboat manned
by members of the crew, he suddenly descried a blacker mass
looming in the darkness and realized that the submarine had
surfaced almost alongside the boat. Everyone expected the

machine guns to cut loose in a moment, but the German, after asking a few questions, went his way.

"When I realized what that thing was," said the old gentleman later, "it flashed into my mind that these sailors were brave men, and I had never before seen brave men suddenly confronted with mortal peril. How would they respond? But watching intently I could see no reaction, except what I can only describe as a white shadow that seemed to cross their faces as the German hailed us. It was a quarter of an hour later that I remembered that, if he had opened fire, I would have been shot, too, and then I was horribly scared."

By the square spectacles of Benjamin Franklin and the chin whiskers of Horace Greeley, there was a newspaperman! And, gray hairs and all, there was a young man.

If, then, it is reasonable to infer that the very fact of his imprisonment behind the bars of language tends to stimulate the journalist's desire for freedom of expression; if his share of the universal human enjoyment of power tends to stimulate it further; and if the satisfaction of his temperamental urges gives it a third impetus, one may logically expect to find in this craftsman a vigilant and vigorous defender of freedom of expression, both for himself and for others.

Such indeed he is. But to assume that this disposes of the matter, leaving no more to be said, is to ignore the defects of the man's qualities, which would be unpardonable negligence. The typical American journalist is certainly an advocate of free speech, but his effectiveness in that role is limited not only by the conditions under which he works, but also to some extent by the very qualities that make him a good journalist.

Consider, first, the inner conviction that beyond the barrier of language there is a wide world of freedom, to which he can make a partial break-through at moments of his highest efficiency. This is a conviction shared by all writers and by most brain workers of any kind. It is, in fact, the vital spark that keeps them alive as brain workers; if they lost it, they would turn to some other form of endeavor. None has ever achieved the escape, but great writers have gone so far toward it as to keep hope renewed; and some are elated and invigorated by the apparent success of the great mathematicians who, abandoning language altogether, seem able to communicate the ineffable by the use of symbols instead of words.

But the moral obligation to be exact increases in weight with the importance of the matter to be communicated; and in measure as a moral obligation increases in weight it becomes harder to handle. When a bum off Skid Row convicted of vagrancy is given ninety days by a police magistrate and is dragged away protesting, a report that he was in a "towering rage" is no very lamentable error, even though some thought he was only mildly indignant. But to say that the President of the United States burst into a "towering rage" at a press conference, when in fact he did no more than express mild displeasure, is enough to get a reporter expelled from such conferences. A wrathful bum affects the well-being only of the policemen who wrestle with him; but a wrathful President might act to the injury of the whole country.

Unfortunately, as every professional knows and, knowing, trembles, it is just when you are most intent on making your communication correspond to truth within the tolerance of a hairsbreadth that you are most likely to perpetrate an abominable lie. The very straining for precision leads to overstatement in one sentence and to understatement in the next, thereby building up a tissue of falsehood. A speaker making an oral report on an important matter labors under the same handicap, which is why no direct newspaper quotation of the President is allowed except by special permission. Under the system of indirect quotation, if a lie gets out, the blame can be laid on the reporter—a justifiable injustice, so to speak, since the President's reputation for veracity is more important than that of any reporter.

It must be taken into account, however, that a writer's effort to escape ambiguity—certainly a virtue—is often self-defeating, circling right back into the vice that is its opposite. So much for the love of liberty of the prisoner of words.

The natural, and laudable, aspiration to be of some account in the world requires no comment. The traps into which overweening ambition may lead a once honest man are familiar to all the world. So much for that.

Even the temperament of the born spectator has its snares for the unwary. They are well illustrated by a shrewd lawyer's estimate not of a newspaperman, but of a judge who shared that temperament. This jurist was denounced furiously by half the bar for half the time; yet he was the author of a series of decisions so brilliant and so correct that they command the admiration of the whole profession.

"It all depends upon the case," said the analytical lawyer. "If it is one in which not only are the facts disputed, but the law itself is vague and obscure, then any slight advantage to one side may be decisive. So from the jump opposing counsel are at each other's throats, fighting bitterly for every fraction of an inch, and doing their level best to put something over on the court itself. In such a case I could not ask for a finer judge than he—impartial, alert, imperturbable, dignified and always completely master of the situation. But if the case is one that drones along for days through piles of musty documents and statistical tables, he just can't take it. Presently he will make a ruling reversing every legal authority from Solon to Hugo Black, knowing better, but compelled to stir things up."

The journalist, one born for the job and therefore first rate, is subject to the same weakness. When dull days possess the earth he is likely to perpetrate something on the order of the famous crime of a Baltimore reporter about 1910. Desperate for some kind of story when there was no story, he rented a bicycle and lurked around a corner until he could mount it and run into the late Cardinal Gibbons, when His Eminence was taking his daily stroll in Charles Street. Reputable journalists shake their heads sadly over such goings-on, but it is not in them to resist pointing out that the fellow got a story, all right.

So much for temperament.

The conclusion of the whole matter is that the very psychological traits that combine to make a man a good journalist are also capable, under some circumstances, of making him a very bad one. The craft, like everything else in life, is shaped by its environment. Freedom of expression is capable of being abused, and its abuse by journalists is as definite a threat to its survival as is its restriction and possible suppression by tyrants.

Taking for granted that there is a reader who has followed the argument to this point, if he now finds himself in a state of uncertainty mingled with some anxiety, the study has served its purpose, for that is where he should be. Freedom of opinion and expression, which includes freedom of the press, has no guaranteed future in the United States and the sooner that fact is faced the better for all concerned.

The press cannot be the guarantor because a free press is the creature, not the creator of freedom. If that were not conclusive, there remains the fact that the press is divided against itself, both by the conditions under which it operates and by the temperamental qualities of its operatives. Potentially it is as effective an instrument of tyranny as of freedom and, as we have seen, some ineradicable influences thrust it in that direction. Since its power is derivative and its direction uncertain the press can hardly be considered an effective guarantor.

As for the Constitution, it is just as strong as the people's approval of its provisions, and no stronger. Its efficiency, in and of itself, is limited to preventing hasty and ill-considered action in a moment of temporary excitement, action that will be repented tomorrow or next week. It does serve that purpose fairly well; but as against a steady, long-continued thrust of public opinion it is only a paper barrier. Consider, if you please, the present value of the guarantee in the Second Amendment: "The right of the people to keep *and bear* arms shall not be infringed." Do not talk of the intervention of the police power of the States. In the District of Columbia, not a State but Federal territory, let a policemen catch you carrying a pistol, or even a switchblade knife, and see how much good that guarantee does you! We cannot rely on the Constitution any more than on the press to protect our liberties.

We cannot rely on anything but ourselves. In the last analysis it is the people who must protect both the press and the Constitution, not the other way about. No nation ever had a free press except one that demanded a free press. No nation ever kept a free press except one that was harshly intolerant of every tendency toward slavishness exhibited by its press. When the opposing forces operating on the press are almost equal, and it wavers uncertainly, then the third force that will tip the scales is the weight of public opinion. When the people are convinced, or even half convinced, that there is something more precious than freedom, you will find a large segment of the press agreeing with them and reinforcing the delusion; but when the people demand liberty first, and peace and prosperity second, then the press becomes a mighty engine for the defense of freedom.

On this showing there would seem to be much justification for the anxiety of those who are persuaded that the survival of freedom is at best an even bet, like the flip of a coin, and at worst much less than even. But this showing leaves out of account two factors, one affecting the press, the other the American public, both of which tend to shift the odds to the favorable.

As regards the press, there is this to be remembered: every influence that sways the journalist, whether a newspaper owner or merely a hired hand, toward the status of a freeman is an influence that engenders pride; and every contrary influence makes him, consciously or subconsciously, apologetic. But the growth of pride tends to accelerate; a small thrust in that direction is likely to acquire rather than lose momentum and any momentary enjoyment of independence by a journalist stimulates his appetite for more. If to enjoyment is added even a mild public approval the stimulus becomes very strong.

It is accordingly easier to encourage freedom than to establish servility in the press. If an equal weight of public opinion were thrown into both sides of the scale, the side of freedom would have the advantage.

PERIL and PROMISE

As regards the public, the apathy so much and so loudly bemoaned at present may be accounted for by factors that do not include a deterioration in the character of the American people. That factor, to be sure, is not excluded. It is quite possible that we may be, on the whole, degenerating into a servile race; but one is not compelled to believe it.

For this is not by any means the first time that pessimists have stood ready to give us up in despair, and to cite shockingly good reasons for their melancholy. Our political history is certainly not that of a people immune to mass hysteria; on the contrary, when one contemplates the long succession of Pied Pipers behind whom we have danced, from Citizen Genêt to Huey Long, it is a temptation to say that we rather specialize in throwing fits of astounding variety and violence.

Our remarkable characteristic, as a nation, is not our resistance to the hocus-pocus of the warlocks and soothsayers, but our recuperative powers which, as a rule, act suddenly and completely. When the American's common sense does reassert itself not only does he cease to believe in the spells and incantations of the witch doctor, but he ceases to believe that he ever believed in them. Our spasms are followed not by repentance in sackcloth and ashes, but by bland forgetfulness. Who was Father Coughlin, anyhow? What was mah-jongg?

It is true that our present apparent indifference to freedom has outlasted any of the earlier seizures, and it is always possible that one of them will carry us past the point of no return. But the causes of this one were also without precedent. Four years of a desperate double war were followed by the rise of problems two of which were more nerve-shattering than any war. These were a sudden weight of responsibility, and a sudden challenge not to our military power, but to our intelligence.

Responsibility for leadership of the free world was first thrown upon us in 1919, and we couldn't bear it. We collapsed and crawled out from under it. We have been doing better this time, but we find it no light burden, even now.

Then Communism, like the jinni from the fisherman's bottle emerging at first as mere smoke, has assumed the shape of a monster filling our intellectual horizon, a giant we cannot subdue by force but only by fast thinking.

No war ever gave us the psychological shock administered by these two. It is no cause for wonder that the effects have lasted longer than those of, say, Know-Nothingism, or the Anti-Masonic craze. The cause for wonder is rather that under such battering the great mass of the American people has retained as much sanity as it still possesses.

So while it would be fatuous to deny that freedom of the mind, which includes freedom of the press, is in peril, to assume that it is doomed is defeatism; and that, too, is fatuous. For there is promise in the very fact that we have stood up under the cold war for twelve long years—not without moral losses, it is true, but without moral disaster. Perhaps the old American love of liberty drowses, like Barbarossa in some